READY TO GO ¹

Language • Lifeskills • Civics

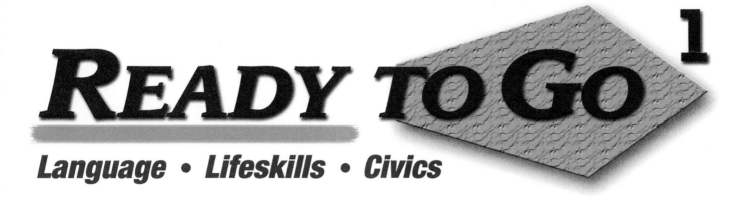

READY TO GO ¹

Language • Lifeskills • Civics

Joan Saslow

Tim Collins

Edwina Hoffman

Series Advisor

Longman

Ready to Go: Language, Lifeskills, Civics 1

Pearson Education, 10 Bank Street, White Plains, NY 10606

Vice president, instructional design: Allen Ascher
Senior acquisitions editor: Marian Wassner
Senior development editor: Marcia Schonzeit
Ready to Go development editor: Julie Rouse
Assistant editor: Patricia Lattanzio
Vice president, director of design and production: Rhea Banker
Executive managing editor: Linda Moser
Senior production editor: Christine Lauricella
Ready to Go production editor: Marc Oliver
Production supervisor: Liza Pleva
Ready to Go production manager: Ray Keating
Senior manufacturing manager: Patrice Fraccio
Manufacturing supervisor: Dave Dickey
Cover design: Ann France
Text design: Ann France
Text composition: Word and Image
Ready to Go text composition: Lehigh Press
Illustrations: Craig Attebery, pp. 36, 37, 45, 46, 61, 74, 81, 82, 110; Crowleart Group, pp. 63, 80, 82, 91, 92, 114, 128-130; Brian Hughes, pp. 1, 4, 26, 27, 31, 33, 34, 36, 38, 39, 41, 43, 46, 48, 49, 50, 51, 56, 58, 60, 70, 73, 75, 79, 87, 97, 108-111, 117, 121; Paul McCusker, pp. 27, 68, 80, 105, 111; Suzanne Mogensen, pp. 2, 15, 20, 25, 33, 40, 52, 53, 62, 66, 86, 88, 91, 100, 114; Tom Newsom, pp. 48, 51, 54, 111; Dusan Petricic, p. 101; Stephen Quinlan, p. 99; NSV Productions, pp. 13, 16, 22, 24, 38, 40, 46, 49, 85, 89, 106, 120, 142; Meryl Treatner, pp. 12, 25, 30, 42, 72, 75, 84, 85, 90, 96, 97, 102, 120, 126; Word & Image Design, pp. 5, 13, 19, 20, 21, 32, 33, 44, 45, 55-58, 61, 68, 69, 70, 73, 81, 82, 89, 93, 94, 104-106, 116-118, 129; Anna Veltfort, pp. 17, 18, 23, 29, 35, 41, 47, 53, 59, 65, 71, 77, 78, 83, 87, 95, 101, 107, 113, 119, 125, 131
Photography: Gilbert Duclos, pp. 2, 3, 6-11, 14, 15, 19, 21, 26, 27, 31, 38, 39, 43, 45, 50, 51, 55, 56, 57, 61, 62, 63, 67, 69, 73, 74, 75, 79, 86, 87, 89, 91, 92, 97, 98, 99, 103, 110, 111, 115, 117, 122, 123, 127, 128; Page 21 © R. Lewine/First Light; page 32 Chronis Jons/Stone; page 85 © J. Henley/First Light

Library of Congress Cataloging-in-Publication Data

Saslow, Joan M.
  Ready to Go : language, lifeskills, civics/ Joan Saslow, Tim Collins.
    p. cm.
  ISBN 0-13-177642-8 (v.1) -- ISBN 0-13-177644-4 (v.2) -- ISBN 0-13-177645-2 (v. 3) -- ISBN 0-13-177646-0 (v4)
    1. English language--Textbooks for foreign speakers. 2. Life skills--Problems, exercises, etc. 3. Civics--Problems, exercises, etc. I. Collins, Tim. II. Title.

PE1128 .S2755 2003
428.2'4--dc21   2002043418

1 2 3 4 5 6 7 8 9 10—WC—08 07 06 05 04 03

Contents

Scope and sequence

Unit	Lifeskills	Grammar	Social Language	Vocabulary	Civics/Culture Concepts
1 **Your life** page 12	• Ask for and give name, occupation, and country of origin • Make introductions • Introduce self	• The present tense of *be*, singular forms	How to • exchange personal information • express sympathy • offer support	• Occupations	• Shake hands and make eye contact. (W)[1] • Jobs are not determined by gender. • It's OK to ask about another's occupation. • Use first names in informal settings. • Use titles and last names in "official" settings.
2 **The community** page 24	• Identify places in the community, workplaces, and places within buildings • Understand and give directions to a place	• The present tense of *be*, plural forms	How to • clarify • politely request directions • initiate a conversation • express thanks • acknowledge thanks	• Workplaces • Places at work • Places in the community	• Be friendly and helpful to others at work. • It's OK to ask strangers for directions. • Assist strangers who ask for help.
3 **Technology** page 26	• Identify common machines • Use and troubleshoot technology • Understand and give instructions for using machines	• Suggestions with *Let's* • Imperatives	How to • express dismay • clarify • suggest a course of action • ask for help • agree to a request • express lack of knowledge	• Common machines and machine parts • Verbs for machine operation	• It's OK to say "I don't know." • Help co-workers to solve problems. • It's OK to ask co-workers for help. • It's OK to tell a supervisor about a problem.
4 **The consumer world** page 48	• Talk about clothes, colors, and sizes • Ask for and offer service • Complain about merchandise • Ask for refunds and exchanges • Fill out order forms and merchandise return forms	• The simple present tense • *This, that, these,* and *those*	How to • express likes and dislikes • state wants and needs • apologize • accept an offer • complain • offer a tentative answer	• Clothing, sizes, and colors	• Salespeople expect to help customers. • Apologize when unable to fulfill a request. • Unsatisfactory merchandise can be returned. • Keep receipts as proof of purchase. • It's important to follow company policy.
5 **Time** page 60	• Ask for and give times, days, and dates • Talk about opening and closing times • Understand work schedules • Understand punctuality	• Impersonal statements with *It's* • Questions with *What time* and *When* • Ordinal numbers	How to • express concern • express approval • express uncertainty • say good-bye	• Times of day, months, days, and years	• It's important to be punctual. • Plan activities to observe work and business schedules and hours.

[1]Welcome Unit

Math Concepts and Practical Math Skills	Critical Thinking Skills	Correlations to National Standards		
		SCANS Competencies	CASAS Life Skill Competencies[2]	EFF Content Standards[3]
• Understand and write numerals 0-100 (W)[1] • Understand and use numbers in addresses and telephone numbers (W)[1] • Count and classify items in a list • Conduct a poll/survey	• Reasoning (classifies)	• Understands social systems • Acquires and evaluates information • Interprets and communicates information • Works well with people of culturally diverse backgrounds	0.1.2, 0.1.4, 0.2.2, 0.2.4, 4.1.1, 4.1.2, 4.1.3, 4.1.6, 4.1.7, 4.1.8, 4.1.9, 4.2.4, 4.3.2, 4.4.1, 4.4.2, 4.4.5, 4.4.6, 4.6.1, 4.6.2, 4.6.3, 4.7.1, 4.7.2, 4.8.1, 4.8.2, 4.8.5, 4.8.6, 4.9.1, 4.9.3	A full range of EFF Content Standards is included in this unit. The following are emphasized: • Read with Understanding 1–4 • Convey Ideas in Writing 3, 4 • Speak So Others Can Understand 1–4 • Listen Actively 1–4 • Take Responsibility for Learning 1–3, 6
• Interpret spatial relationships	• Reasoning (makes inferences)	• Understands social and organizational systems • Acquires and evaluates information • Interprets and communicates information	0.1.2, 0.1.3, 0.1.5, 0.2.3, 0.2.4, 1.1.3, 1.3.7, 1.9.4, 1.9.6, 2.2.1, 2.2.5, 2.5.2, 2.5.3, 2.5.4, 2.6.1, 5.6.1, 5.6.4	A full range of EFF Content Standards is included in this unit. The following are emphasized: • Read with Understanding 1–4 • Speak So Others Can Understand 1–4 • Listen Actively 1–4 • Observe Critically 1–5 • Advocate and Influence 1-5
• Follow sequential instructions	• Reasoning (applies knowledge to new situations)	• Uses technology • Acquires and evaluates information • Interprets and communicates information	0.1.2, 0.1.3, 0.1.5, 0.2.3, 0.2.4, 1.4.1, 1.7.3, 1.7.4, 1.7.5, 2.1.6, 2.1.8, 4.3.1, 4.3.3, 4.4.3, 4.4.8, 4.5.1, 4.5.4, 4.5.5, 4.5.6, 4.5.7, 4.9.4	A full range of EFF Content Standards is included in this unit. The following are emphasized: • Observe Critically 1–5 • Solve Problems and Make Decisions 1–6 • Cooperate with Others 1–4 • Guide Others 1–4 • Take Responsibility for Learning 1–3, 5, 6
• Understand numerical and relative sizes • Read receipts and understand prices, discounts, sum of prices, tax, and total	• Decision-making (evaluates and chooses the best alternative)	• Serves customers • Works toward agreement • Acquires and evaluates information • Interprets and communicates information	0.1.2, 0.1.4, 0.1.5, 0.2.3, 0.2.4, 1.1.9, 1.2.1, 1.2.5, 1.3.1, 1.3.3, 1.3.7, 1.3.9, 1.6.3, 1.7.2, 4.8.3, 4.8.4, 4.8.5, 4.8.6, 7.3.1, 7.3.2, 8.1.2, 8.1.4	A full range of EFF Content Standards is included in this unit. The following are emphasized: • Read with Understanding 1–4 • Convey Ideas in Writing 1–4 • Observe Critically 1–5 • Solve Problems and Make Decisions 1–6 • Advocate and Influence 1–5 • Guide Others 1–4 • Take Responsibility for Learning 1–3, 5, 6
• Tell time • Understand and use cardinal and ordinal numbers in dates • Interpret and compare schedules	• Reasoning (makes inferences and draws conclusions) • Decision-making (evaluates and chooses the best alternative)	• Allocates time • Acquires and evaluates information • Interprets and communicates information • Understands social and organizational systems	0.1.2, 0.1.5, 0.2.3, 0.2.4, 2.1.3, 2.2.4, 2.3.1, 2.3.2, 2.6.2, 2.7.1, 3.1.2	A full range of EFF Content Standards is included in this unit. The following are emphasized: • Convey Ideas in Writing 2–4 • Observe Critically 1–5 • Use Math to Solve Problems and Communicate 2, 3, 5 • Plan 1, 2, 4, 5 • Learn Through Research 1–3

[1]Welcome Unit

[2]The corresponding CASAS Life Skill Competency List is available at **www.longman.com/readytogo**.

[3]A more extensive correlation to EFF Content Standards is available at **www.longman.com/readytogo**.

Unit	Lifeskills	Grammar	Social Language	Vocabulary	Civics/Culture Concepts
6 **Supplies and services** page 72	• Talk about food • Write shopping lists • Use supplies appropriately • Give and follow instructions	• Count/non-count noun distinction • Questions with *How many* and *How much* • Impersonal statements with *There is / There are*	How to • start a conversation • respond to a greeting • ask for additional information • solicit an opinion • agree and disagree	• Common foods and drinks • Cooking verbs	• It's OK to ask people about their tastes. • It's important to plan ahead.
7 **Relationships** page 84	• Talk about abilities and responsibilities • Ask for and give reasons • Understand company policies regarding time off • Request a personal day	• The present continuous • *Can* and *Have to* • Questions with *Why* • Statements with *because*	How to • ask for and give reasons • state an obligation • give and accept excuses	• Family members • Action verbs	• Apologize and give a reason when unable to do something. • Express sympathy for another's misfortune. • Be willing to help out when an employer is short-handed.
8 **Health and safety** page 96	• Describe symptoms and injuries • Make healthcare appointments • Call 911 • Report accidents, injuries, and illnesses at work • Read and write dates in numbers	• Possessives • Contrast of the simple present tense and the present continuous	How to • conduct a phone conversation • accept an apology • offer to call back later • make an appointment • express sympathy • offer good wishes • express appreciation	• Parts of the body • Common illnesses and injuries	• Understand and use telephone etiquette. • Express concern when someone is ill or hurt. • It's a duty to call 911 in an emergency.
9 **Money** page 108	• Make and accept payment with cash, check, and credit card • Count money and make change • Provide service • Write checks • Show I.D. upon request	• The future with *be going to* • Questions with *Whose*	How to • ask for change • offer to check something • inquire about a price • ask for time to consider a purchase • agree to make a purchase	• Coin and bill names • Forms of payment • Payment verbs	• It's OK to ask about prices. • I.D. is required when paying with a personal check. • Businesses have the right to determine types of payment accepted.
10 **Your career** page 120	• Interview for a job • Talk about jobs, skills, and experience • Read help-wanted ads • Complete a job application	• The past tense of *be* • The simple past tense of regular and irregular verbs	How to • convince • clarify	• Occupations • Employment skills	• Arrive on time for a job interview. • Appropriate dress and grooming are essential in an interview. • Address an interviewer by title and last name.

Math Concepts and Practical Math Skills	Critical Thinking Skills	Correlations to National Standards		
		SCANS Competencies	CASAS Life Skill Competencies[1]	EFF Content Standards[2]
• Understand quantities and containers • Understand measurements in recipes • Follow sequential directions • Compare quantities in recipes with available supplies	• Decision-making (evaluates and chooses the best alternative) • Reasoning (sequences, draws conclusions)	• Allocates resources • Understands organizational systems • Participates as a member of a team • Acquires and evaluates information • Interprets and communicates information • Serves customers • Teaches others	0.1.2, 0.1.5, 0.2.3, 0.2.4, 1.1.1, 1.1.6, 1.2.2, 1.2.5, 1.3.8, 1.6.1, 3.5.1, 3.5.2, 3.5.3	A full range of EFF Content Standards is included in this unit. The following are emphasized: • Convey Ideas in Writing 1–4 • Listen Actively 1–4 • Observe Critically 1–5 • Guide Others 1–3 • Take Responsibility for Learning 1–3, 5, 6
• Estimate time needed to accomplish tasks • Use schedules to manage time and commitments • Calculate when to request a personal day based on company policy	• Decision-making (evaluates and chooses the best alternative)	• Understands social and organizational systems • Acquires and evaluates information • Interprets and communicates information • Negotiates	0.1.2, 0.1.5, 0.2.3, 0.2.4	A full range of EFF Content Standards is included in this unit. The following are emphasized: • Solve Problems and Make Decisions 1–3, 5, 6 • Plan 1–5 • Take Responsibility for Learning 1–3, 5, 6
• Schedule appointments • Express dates in numbers based on understanding of sequence	• Reasoning (makes inferences and draws conclusions)	• Acquires and evaluates information • Interprets and communicates information • Understands social and organizational systems	0.1.2, 0.1.5, 0.2.3, 0.2.4, 1.9.7, 2.1.2, 2.1.7, 2.1.8, 2.5.1, 2.5.2, 2.5.3, 3.1.1, 3.1.2, 3.1.3, 3.2.1, 3.3.1, 3.3.2, 3.3.3, 3.4.2, 3.4.3, 3.5.4, 4.3.2, 4.3.3, 4.3.4, 5.3.8	A full range of EFF Content Standards is included in this unit. The following are emphasized: • Convey Ideas in Writing 1–4 • Listen Actively 1–4 • Solve Problems and Make Decisions 1, 3, 4, 6 • Advocate and Influence 1–3, 5 • Take Responsibility for Learning 1–4, 6
• Understand values of U.S. currency • Calculate combinations of coins and bills that equal a stated price or amount • Make change • State prices • Interpret bills and receipts	• Knowing how to learn (takes notes)	• Allocates money • Serves customers • Acquires and evaluates information • Interprets and communicates information	0.1.2, 0.1.5, 0.2.3, 0.2.4, 1.1.6, 1.2.2, 1.2.3, 1.2.4, 1.2.5, 1.3.2, 1.3.3, 1.3.4, 1.3.6, 1.5.1, 1.5.2, 1.5.3, 1.8.1, 1.8.2, 1.8.3, 1.8.4, 1.8.5, 1.9.2, 2.5.7, 2.6.4, 4.2.1, 4.7.1, 5.4.2, 5.8.1, 5.8.2, 5.8.3, 6.0.1, 6.0.2, 6.0.3	A full range of EFF Content Standards is included in this unit. The following are emphasized: • Convey Ideas in Writing 1–4 • Speak So Others Can Understand 1–4 • Listen Actively 1–4 • Use Math to Solve Problems and Communicate 1–5
• Compare required work hours at potential jobs with hours of availability	• Reasoning (makes associations) • Decision-making (evaluates and chooses the best alternative)	• Acquires and evaluates information • Interprets and communicates information	0.1.2, 0.1.5, 0.2.3, 0.2.4, 4.1.2, 4.1.3, 4.1.4, 4.1.5, 4.1.6, 4.1.7, 4.2.4, 4.3.2, 4.4.1, 4.4.2, 4.4.4, 4.4.5, 4.4.6, 4.4.7, 4.4.8, 4.6.1, 4.6.2, 4.6.3, 4.6.4, 4.6.5, 4.7.1, 4.7.2, 4.7.3, 4.7.4, 4.8.1, 4.8.5, 4.8.6, 4.9.3, 4.9.4	A full range of EFF Content Standards is included in this unit. The following are emphasized: • Observe Critically 1–5 • Advocate and Influence 1–5 • Take Responsibility for Learning 1, 3, 4, 6

[1]The corresponding CASAS Life Skill Competency List is available at **www.longman.com/readytogo**.
[2]A more extensive correlation to EFF Content Standards is available at **www.longman.com/readytogo**.

Acknowledgments

The authors wish to acknowledge with gratitude the following consultants and reviewers —our partners in the development of *Ready to Go*.

Regional Consultant Board

The following people have participated on an ongoing basis in shaping the content and approach of *Ready to Go*:

Ann Belletire, Northern Illinois University–Business and Industry Services, Oak Brook, Illinois • **Sandra Bergman**, Instructional Facilitator, Alternative, Adult, and Continuing Education Program, New York City Board of Education • **Sherie Burnette**, Assistant Dean, Workforce Education, Brookhaven College of the Dallas County Community College District, Farmers Branch, Texas • **Michael Feher**, Boston Chinatown Neighborhood Center, Boston, Massachusetts • **Susan B. Kanter**, Instructional Supervisor, Continuing Education and Contract Training, Houston Community College-Southwest, Houston, Texas • **Brigitte Marshall**, Consultant, Albany, California • **Monica Oliva**, Educational Specialist, Miami-Dade County Public Schools, Miami, Florida • **Mary E. O'Neill**, Coordinator of Community Education, ESL, Northern Virginia Community College-Annandale Campus, Annandale, Virginia • **Grace Tanaka**, Professor of ESL, Santa Ana College School of Continuing Education; ESL Facilitator, Centennial Education Center, Santa Ana, California • **Marcia L. Taylor**, Workplace Instructor, Joblink, Ispat-Inland Inc., East Chicago, Indiana

Reviewers

The following people shared their perspectives and made suggestions either by reviewing manuscript or participating in editorial conferences with the authors and editors:

Leslie Jo Adams, Santa Ana College–Centennial Education Center, Santa Ana, California • **Sandra Anderson**, El Monte-Rosemead Adult School, El Monte, California • **Marcy Berquist**, San Diego Community College District, San Diego, California • **Ruth Brigham**, A.C.C.E.S.S., Boston, Massachusetts • **Donna Burns**, Mt. San Antonio College, Walnut, California • **Eric Burton**, Downington Area School District, Downington, Pennsylvania • **Michael James Climo**, West Los Angeles College, Culver City, California • **Teresa Costa**, The English Center, Miami, Florida • **Robert Cote**, Miami-Dade County Public Schools, Miami, Florida • **Georgette Davis**, North Orange County Community College District, Orange County, California • **Janet Ennis**, Santa Ana College–Centennial Education Center, Santa Ana, California • **Peggy Fergus**, Northern Illinois University–Business and Industry Services, Oak Brook, Illinois • **Oliva Fernandez**, Hillsborough County Public Schools–Adult & Community Education, Tampa, Florida • **Elizabeth Fitzgerald**, Hialeah Adult & Community Center, Hialeah, Florida • **Marty Furch**, Palomar College, San Diego, California • **Eric Glicker**, North Orange County Community College District, Orange County, California • **Steve Gwynne**, San Diego Community College District, San Diego, California • **Victoria Hathaway**, DePaul University, Chicago, Illinois • **Jeffrey L. Janulis**, Richard J. Daley College, City Colleges of Chicago, Chicago, Illinois • **Mary Karamourtopoulos**, Northern Essex Community College, Haverhill, Massachusetts • **Shirley Kelly**, Brookhaven College of the Dallas County Community College District, Farmers Branch, Texas • **Marilou Kessler**, Jewish Vocational Service–Vocational English Program, Chicago, Illinois • **Henry Kim**, North Orange County Community College District, Orange County, California • **Dr. Maria H. Koonce**, Broward County Public Schools, Ft. Lauderdale, Florida • **John Kostovich**, South Texas Community College–Intensive English Program, McAllen, Texas • **Jacques LaCour**, Mt. Diablo Adult Education, Concord, California • **Beatrice Liebman**, Miami Sunset Adult Center, Miami, Florida • **Doris Lorden**, Wright College–Workforce Training Center, Chicago, Illinois • **Mike Lowman**, Coral Gables Adult Education Center, Coral Gables, Florida • **Lois Maharg**, Delaware Technical and Community College • **Vicki Moore**, El Monte-Rosemead Adult School, El Monte, California • **Deborah Nash**, School Board of Palm Beach County Schools, West Palm Beach, Florida • **Cindy Neubrech**, Mt. San Antonio College, Walnut, California • **Patricia Peabody**, Broward County Public Schools, Ft. Lauderdale, Florida • **Joe A. Perez**, Hillsborough County Public Schools, Tampa, Florida • **Diane Pinkley**, Teacher's College, Columbia University, New York, New York • **Kay Powell**, Santa Ana College–Centennial Education Center, Santa Ana, California • **Wendy Rader**, San Diego Community College District, San Diego, California • **Don Robison**, Jewish Vocational Service–Workplace Literacy, Chicago, Illinois • **Richard Sasso**, Triton College, River Grove, Illinois • **Mary Segovia**, El Monte-Rosemead Adult School, El Monte, California • **Laurie Shapero**, Miami-Dade Community College, Miami, Florida • **Sara Shapiro**, El Monte-Rosemead Adult School, El Monte, California • **Samanthia Spence**, Richland College, Dallas, Texas • **JoAnn Stehy**, North Orange County Community College District, Orange County, California • **Margaret Teske**, Mt. San Antonio College, Walnut, California • **Dung Tran**, North Orange County Community College District, Orange County, California • **Claire Valier**, School District of Palm Beach County, West Palm Beach, Florida • **Catherine M. Waterman**, Rancho Santiago Community College, Santa Ana, California • **James Wilson**, Mt. San Antonio College, Walnut, California

To the teacher

Ready to Go: Language, Lifeskills, Civics is a four-level, standards-based course in English as a second language. *Ready to Go* prepares adults for self-sufficiency in the three principal areas of their lives: the community, the home, and the workplace.

Communicative competence in English is of critical importance in achieving self-sufficiency. *Ready to Go* applies the best of current second language acquisition research to ensure immediate success, rapidly enabling learners to

- understand the spoken and written language of daily life.
- communicate orally and in writing.
- understand the culture and civic expectations of their new environment.
- master lifeskills necessary to survive and thrive in the American community and workplace.

To achieve these goals with efficiency and speed, *Ready to Go* weaves together three integrated strands: language, lifeskills, and civics*, tightly correlating the major state and federal standards with a complete language syllabus and relevant social language.

Course Length

Ready to Go is designed to be used in a period of 60 to 90 classroom hours. This period can be shortened or lengthened, based on the needs of the group or the program. The Teacher's Edition gives detailed instructions for tailoring *Ready to Go* to specific settings, circumstances, and student groups.

Components
Student's Book

The *Ready to Go* Student's Book is a complete four-skills text, integrating listening, speaking, reading, and writing, with lifeskills, math skills, civics concepts, and authentic practice understanding native speech and real-life documents. The book contains 10 units, each one followed by a concise review section. For lesson planning and compliance with curriculum guidelines, the Scope and Sequence chart (on pages vi–ix) clearly spells out the following elements for each unit:

- lifeskills
- grammar
- social language
- vocabulary
- civics/culture concepts
- math concepts and practical math skills
- critical thinking skills
- SCANS Competencies
- CASAS Life Skill Competencies
- EFF Content Standards

Further correlations of state and local standards to the *Ready to Go* course can be downloaded at no cost from the *Ready to Go* companion website at www.longman.com/ready to go.

In order to facilitate student-centered instruction, *Ready to Go* uses a variety of grouping strategies: pairs, groups, and whole class. In numerous activities, learners work with others to create a joint product. Those activities are labeled collaborative activities.

*In *Ready to Go*, the term "civics" refers to concepts that introduce learners to expected social behavior in this culture, an understanding of which is essential *before* students can participate fully or truly understand their rights and responsibilities as citizens. The term does not refer to citizenship education.

Two special features of the *Ready to Go* Student's Book are <u>Do it yourself!</u> and <u>Authentic practice</u>.

Because learners have an immediate need to use their new language outside the class, <u>Do it yourself!</u> provides a daily opportunity for students of diverse abilities to put new language into their own words. This affords them a chance to "try their wings" in the safe and supportive environment of the classroom.

<u>Authentic practice</u> activities create a "living language laboratory" within the classroom. Learners practice responding to authentic models of spoken and written English with the limited language they know. In this way, students build their confidence and skill in coping with the language of the real world.

Audiocassettes

Because listening comprehension is a fundamental survival and success skill for new speakers of English, *Ready to Go* includes a comprehensive listening strand in each unit of the Student's Book. In addition to listening comprehension activities, there are numerous other opportunities for learners to practice their listening skills. All exercises that appear on audiocassette are marked with a 🎧 symbol. A transcript of each listening comprehension activity is located on its corresponding Teacher's Edition page, for easy reference.

Teacher's Edition

An interleaved Teacher's Edition provides page-by-page teaching suggestions that add value to the Student's Book. In addition to general and day-by-day teaching suggestions, each teacher's page includes optional activities, language and culture notes that will help teachers demystify and explain new language to students, answers to all exercises, and the tapescript of each listening comprehension activity.

Workbook

In addition to the ample opportunities for reading and writing practice contained in the Student's Book, the *Ready to Go* Workbook contains further reading and writing exercises. The Workbook is valuable for homework or for in-class activities. An added feature is a test preparation activity for each unit, which readies learners for "bubbling in" and coping with the formats of standardized language tests.

Teacher's Resource Binder

A three-ring binder contains a wealth of valuable items to enable busy teachers to customize their instruction and make the preparation of supplementary teaching aids unnecessary. The Classroom Booster Pack provided with the Binder features pair-work cards, vocabulary flash cards, grammar self-checks, photo chat cards, and extension activities for daily use. Also included in the Binder are the following additional teacher support materials: Correlations of *Ready to Go* with state and federal standards, Student Progress Checklists, Pre- and Post-Tests and Achievement Tests, and Skills for Test Taking.

Placement Test

A simple-to-administer test places students accurately within the *Ready to Go* series.

Ready to Go Companion Website

The *Ready to Go* companion website (www.longman.com/readytogo) provides numerous additional resources for students and teachers. This no-cost, high-benefit feature includes opportunities for further practice of language and content from the *Ready to Go* Student's Book. For the teacher, there are optional strategies and materials that amplify the *Ready to Go* Teacher's Edition.

Student's Book unit contents
Each unit in the *Ready to Go* Student's Book uses an integrated five-step approach.

1. Vocabulary
   Essential vocabulary is presented in a picture dictionary format and followed by exercises.

2. Practical conversations
   Simple, memorable model conversations that are transferable to learners' own lives permit intensive practice of vocabulary and key social language. These are followed by lively pair-work activities.

3. Practical grammar
   Essential grammatical structure practice enables learners to manipulate the vocabulary and practical conversations to express ideas of their own.

4. Authentic practice 1
   A unique, real-world listening and speaking rehearsal, in which learners build their confidence and ability to interact in the world beyond the classroom.

5. Authentic practice 2
   A unique, real-world reading and writing rehearsal, in which learners build their confidence and skill to understand and use authentic documents that they will encounter in their own lives.

Review
Following each unit is a two-page review for learners to check their progress.

About the authors and series advisor

Authors

Joan Saslow

Joan Saslow has taught English as a second language and English as a foreign language to adults and young adults in the United States and Chile. She taught workplace English at the General Motors auto assembly plant in Tarrytown, NY; and Adult ESL at Westchester Community College and at Marymount College in New York. In addition, Ms. Saslow taught English and French at the Binational Centers of Valparaíso and Viña del Mar, Chile, and the Catholic University of Valparaíso.

Ms. Saslow is the series director of Longman's popular five-level adult series *True Colors, an EFL Course for Real Communication* and of *True Voices*, a five-level video course. She is the author of *English in Context: Reading Comprehension for Science and Technology*, a three-level series for English for special purposes. In addition, Ms. Saslow has been an editor of language teaching materials, a teacher trainer, and a frequent speaker at gatherings of ESL and EFL teachers for over thirty years.

Tim Collins

Tim Collins has taught English as a second language and English as a foreign language to adults and young adults in the United States, Spain, and Morocco. He taught English for special purposes at the Intensive English Institute of the University of Illinois at Urbana. Dr. Collins also taught high school ESL at Lycée Al Badissi, Al Hoceima, Morocco, and advanced English composition at the University of Barcelona. In addition, he taught college Spanish at the University of Illinois at Urbana.

Dr. Collins is Assistant Professor of Language Minority Education at National-Louis University in Chicago, where he teaches in a teacher training program. In addition, he has been a writer and editor of English as a second language and adult education materials for over twelve years. He is a frequent speaker at professional ESL meetings. Dr. Collins's Ph.D. degree is from the University of Texas at Austin.

Series advisor

Edwina Hoffman

Edwina Hoffman has taught English for speakers of other languages in South Florida and at the Miccosukee Tribe of Indians, and English as a foreign language in Venezuela. She provided teacher training in a seven-state area for federally funded multi-functional resource centers serving the southeastern part of the United States. Dr. Hoffman taught English composition at Florida International University and graduate ESOL methods at the University of Miami.

Dr. Hoffman is an instructional supervisor with the adult and vocational programs of Miami-Dade County Public Schools in Miami, Florida. She has acted as a consultant, reviewer, and author of adult ESOL materials for over twenty years. A graduate of Middlebury College, Dr. Hoffman's doctoral degree is from Florida International University.

Welcome to *Ready to Go*

 Vocabulary

Classroom actions

 A. Look at the pictures. Listen.

listen

read

talk

repeat

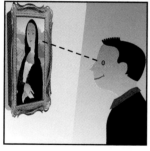

look

point

circle

write

 B. Listen again and repeat.

 C. Now listen and point to the pictures.

D. Look and write.

| write | ~~read~~ | listen | point |

1. _read_

2. _____

3. _____

4. _____

▶ Practical conversations

🎧 A. Listen and read.

B. Listen again and repeat.

C. Pair work.

> **A:** Hello. I'm _____.
> **B:** Hi, _____. I'm _____.
> **A:** Nice to meet you, _____.
> **B:** Nice to meet you too.

Conversation 2   More greetings and introductions

A. Listen and read.

B. Listen again and repeat.

C. Group work.

> **A:** _____, this is _____.
> _____, this is _____.
> **B:** Hi, _____. Nice to meet you.
> **C:** Nice to meet you too.

Vocabulary

Classroom words

A. Look at the pictures. Listen.

a number

a letter

a word

a sentence

B. Listen again and repeat.

C. Read and write.

1. Write a number. _____

2. Write a letter. _____

3. Circle the word: s   12   and

More classroom words

A. Look at the pictures. Listen.

a picture

a book

a teacher   a class

a partner   a partner

classmates

B. Listen again and repeat.

C. Look and point.

1. Point to a book.
2. Point to a picture in the classroom.

Names and addresses

A. Look and listen.

a name

Jeffrey Chang

an address

76 King Street, Watertown, CT   06795

a zip code

(203) 555-3222

a phone number

B. Listen again and repeat.

C. Read and write.

1. Write your name. _____
2. Write your address. _____
3. Write your zip code. _____

The alphabet

A. Listen and read.

Aa	Bb	Cc	Dd	Ee	Ff	Gg	Hh	Ii
Jj	Kk	Ll	Mm	Nn	Oo	Pp	Qq	Rr
Ss	Tt	Uu	Vv	Ww	Xx	Yy	Zz	

B. Listen again and repeat.

Conversations 1 and 2   Spelling names

A. Listen and read.

B. Listen again and repeat.

C. Pair work. **Ask about spelling a name.**

A: Hi, I'm _____.

B: _____. Is that _____?

A: _____.

A. Listen and read.

B. Listen again and repeat.

C. Pair work. **Ask a classmate.**

> **A:** What's your name, please?
> **B:** _____.
> **A:** Is that your first name?
> **B:** Yes, it is.
> **A:** And what's your last name?
> **B:** My last name is _____.
> **A:** Thank you, _____.

Vocabulary

Numbers 0–10

 A. Listen and read.

0	zero	**4**	four	**8**	eight
1	one	**5**	five	**9**	nine
2	two	**6**	six	**10**	ten
3	three	**7**	seven		

 B. Listen again and repeat.

Practical conversation

Conversation   Addresses

A. Listen and read.

B. Listen again and repeat.

Vocabulary

Numbers 11–100

 A. Listen and read.

11	eleven	21	twenty-one	31	thirty-one
12	twelve	22	twenty-two	40	forty
13	thirteen	23	twenty-three	50	fifty
14	fourteen	24	twenty-four	60	sixty
15	fifteen	25	twenty-five	70	seventy
16	sixteen	26	twenty-six	80	eighty
17	seventeen	27	twenty-seven	90	ninety
18	eighteen	28	twenty-eight	100	one hundred
19	nineteen	29	twenty-nine		
20	twenty	30	thirty		

B. Listen again and repeat.

Practical conversations

Conversation 1　More addresses

A. Listen and read.

B. Listen again and repeat.

C. Pair work. Ask your partner for an address.

A: What's your address?
B: _____.
A: _____.
B: You're welcome.

Conversation 2   Telephone numbers and area codes

A. Listen and read.

B. Listen again and repeat.

C. Pair work. Ask your partner for a telephone number.

A: What's your phone number?
B: _____.
A: And your area code?
B: _____.

Create conversations. Use your <u>own</u> words.

Introduce two classmates.

Ask about first name and last name.

Ask about spelling a name.

Ask for an address.

Ask for a telephone number.

Your life

 Vocabulary

Picture dictionary

Objectives

Talk about
- names
- occupations
- where you are from

A. Listen.

Occupations

① a plumber	⑤ a manager	⑨ a bus driver
② a homemaker	⑥ a housekeeper	⑩ a mechanic
③ a cook	⑦ a teacher	⑪ an engineer
④ a cashier	⑧ a student	⑫ an electrician

B. Listen again and repeat.

C. Now listen and point to the pictures.

 How to say it

a teacher   an electrician

D. Write the occupations. Use the words from the box.

a cashier	a plumber	a teacher	a manager
a bus driver	a cook	~~an engineer~~	a mechanic

1. _an engineer_

2. _____

3. _____

4. _____

5. _____

6. _____

7. _____

8. _____

➤ Do it yourself!

Write.

Your occupation: _____

Practical conversations

🎧 **A.** **Listen and read.**

    A: Are you Ken Wang?
    B: Yes, I am.
    A: Oh, hi, Ken. Nice to meet you.
       I'm Luis Lopez.

    A: Are you Ana?
    C: No, I'm not. I'm Marie. Marie Laporte.
    A: Oh, hi, Marie. Good to meet you.
       I'm Luis Lopez.

🎧 **Greetings**
Nice to meet you.
Good to meet you.

🎧 **B.** **Listen again and repeat.**

C. Pair work. **Now use your <u>own</u> names.**

    A: Are you _____?
    B: _____.
    A: Oh, hi, _____. Good to meet you. I'm _____.

🎧 **A.** **Listen and read.**

    A: Where are you from?
    B: China. What about you?
    A: I'm from Mexico.

🎧 **B.** **Listen again and repeat.**

C. Pair work. **Now talk about your <u>own</u> countries.**

    A: Where are you from?
    B: _____. What about you?
    A: I'm from _____.

A. Listen and read.

> A: What do you do?
> B: I'm a mechanic. And you?
> A: I'm a cashier. But right now
>   I'm unemployed.
> B: Oh, I'm sorry. Well, good luck!
> A: Thanks!

B. Listen again and repeat.

C. Pair work. Now use your <u>own</u> occupations.

> A: What do you do?
> B: I'm _____. And you?
> A: I'm _____.

➤ Do it yourself!

Complete the chart. Talk to two students. Ask:

- What's your name?
- Where are you from?
- What do you do?

I'm Maria.
I'm from Mexico.
I'm a bus driver.

Name	From	Occupation
Maria	Mexico	bus driver
1.		
2.		

The verb <u>be</u>

I **am**		
You **are**		
He **is**	a cook.	
She **is**		
Marta **is**		

I **am**		
You **are**		
He **is**	**not** a teacher.	
She **is**		
Marta **is**		

Contractions

I + am	= I'm
you + are	= you're
he + is	= he's
she + is	= she's
Marta + is	= Marta's

A. Complete the sentences. Write <u>am</u>, <u>are</u>, or <u>is</u>.

1. Yuri ___*is*___ from Russia.
2. You _____ a student.
3. He _____ unemployed.
4. I _____ not an engineer.
5. She _____ not from Greece.
6. Blanca _____ my partner.

B. Write about the pictures. Write <u>He's</u> or <u>She's</u>. Write <u>a</u> or <u>an</u>.

1. _She's an engineer._

2. _He's a cashier._

3. _____

4. _____

Questions and short answers with be

Is she	a teacher?	Yes, she is. / No, she's not.
Is he		Yes, he is. / No, he's not.

🎧 Contractions

I am + not	=	I'm not
you are + not	=	you're not
he is + not	=	he's not
she is + not	=	she's not
Marta is + not	=	Marta's not

C. **Complete each conversation. Circle the letter.**

1. **A:** Are you a cashier?
   B: _____
   a. No, I'm not.   **b.** Yes, he is.

2. **A:** Is Rosa from California?
   B: _____
   a. Rosa.   **b.** Yes, she is.

3. **A:** _____
   B: No, she's not.
   a. Is he a plumber?   **b.** Is she a plumber?

4. **A:** _____
   B: Yes, I am.
   a. Are you a student?   **b.** Is he a student?

➤ Do it yourself!

A. **Pair work. Point. Talk about the people. Ask and answer questions.**

A: *Is he an electrician?*
B: *No, he's a manager.*

B. **Personalization. Now tell your partner about yourself.**

I'm a homemaker.

Authentic practice 1

With words you know, YOU can talk to this clerk.

🎧 A. Listen and read.

Clerk: May I help you, please?

YOU *Yes, thank you. I'm Kathy Carter.*

Clerk: Is that Kathy with a C or with a K?

YOU *A K.*

Clerk: And what's your occupation, Ms. Carter?

YOU *I'm a cashier right now.*

Clerk: And are you from Parkville?

YOU *Yes, I am.*

Clerk: OK, good. Please fill out this form.

🎧 B. Listen to the clerk. Read your part.

🎧 C. Listen and read. Choose your response. Circle the letter.

1. "May I help you, please?"
   a. You're welcome.   **b.** Yes, thanks.

2. "Is that with an R?"
   a. Yes.   **b.** Thank you.

3. "What's your occupation?"
   a. I'm a mechanic.   **b.** I'm from China.

🎧 D. Listen. Choose your response. Circle the letter.

1. **a.** I'm from Mexico.   **b.** Well, good luck.

2. **a.** Kathy Carter.   **b.** I'm a cashier.

3. **a.** No, I'm not.   **b.** Yes, thank you.

A. Look at the forms. Listen to the conversations.

1.

CENTRAL HOTEL • Employment Application

NAME: _Dumont_   _Cara_   OCCUPATION: _____
  Last Name   First Name

2.

Employment Application   **ACE COMPANY**   Date: _11/13/02_

NAME: _Lobo_   _Carlos_   OCCUPATION: _____
  Last Name   First Name

ADDRESS: _521 Green St._   _San Francisco_   _CA_   _94114_
  Number and Street   City   State   ZIP Code

3.

🌱 **Garden Street Adult School**   DATE: _2/24/01_

NAME: _____ _Ivan_ _____
  Last Name   First Name

ADDRESS: _76 Low Street_   _Seattle_   _WA_   _98109_
  Number and Street   City   State   ZIP Code

TELEPHONE: (_205_) _555-2156_   NATIONALITY: _Russian_

OCCUPATION: _Taxi driver_   COURSE: _Beginning English_

B. Now listen again and complete the forms.

▶ Do it yourself!

A. Write your <u>own</u> response. Then read your conversation out loud with a partner.

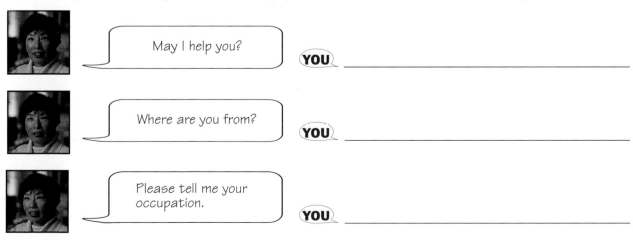

May I help you?   **YOU** _____

Where are you from?   **YOU** _____

Please tell me your occupation.   **YOU** _____

B. Discussion. Talk about another student or about a person at work.

Authentic practice 2

Reading

A. Look at the list of workers.

Bedford Hotel

Current Employees

Cruz, Pilar	**driver**	Rahman, Lisa	**cook**
Hong, Peggy	**cook**	Solano, Cristina	**housekeeper**
Lee, Min	**housekeeper**	Thomas, David	**driver**
Mendoza, Ines	**housekeeper**	Vargas, Juan	**housekeeper**
Metz, Paul	**cook**	Yu, Bryan	**manager**

B. Check ☑ <u>yes</u> or <u>no</u>.

	yes	no
1. The list is from the Bedford Hospital.	☐	☐
2. The list is from the Bedford Hotel.	☐	☐

C. Critical thinking. Read the list.
Write the number of people.

1. ____3____ cooks

2. _____ housekeepers

3. _____ drivers

4. _____ manager

🎧 **How to say it**

a student   student**s**

D. Collaborative activity. Make a chart of the students in <u>your</u> class.
Write the occupations. Write the number of students.

Occupations	Number of students
taxi drivers	*2*

A. Look at the picture. Then answer the questions.

Tania Soto
Assistant Manager

New assistant manager for Bedford

Please welcome Tania Soto to the Bedford Hotel. Tania's a new assistant manager. She's from Puebla, Mexico. She speaks both Spanish and English. In Puebla, Tania was an assistant manager in the Palace Hotel. Tania says, "I'm really happy to be at the Bedford Hotel!"

Good luck in your new job, Tania!

1. What's her name? _____

2. What's her occupation? _____

B. Now read the article. Answer the questions. Write _yes_ or _no_.

1. Is Tania from Mexico? _____

2. Is she a cook? _____

3. Is she unemployed right now? _____

➤ Do it yourself!   A plan-ahead project

A. Discussion. Bring a picture of yourself to class. Talk about the picture with your partner.

B. Show your partner's picture to the class. Tell the class about your partner.

C. Now write about your partner.

NEW Student News

Please welcome _____

to our English class. _____

is from _____.

_____ is _____.

Antonio Costa
Brazil
cook

Marcella Matos
Philippines
nurse

Cristina Romero
Nicaragua
homemaker

Igor Makarov
Russia
taxi driver

A. Vocabulary. Look at the pictures. Write occupations from the box. Write <u>a</u> or <u>an</u>.

cashier	electrician	bus driver	plumber

1. _____

2. _____

3. _____

4. _____

B. Vocabulary. Write <u>your</u> occupation. _____

C. Conversation. Choose <u>your</u> response. Circle the letter.

1. "What do you do?"
   a. I'm a bus driver.   **b.** Mexico.

2. "Where are you from?"
   a. China.   **b.** Nice to meet you.

3. "Is Ivan from Mexico?"
   a. No, he's not.   **b.** He's a bus driver.

4. "Good luck."
   a. I'm sorry.   **b.** Thank you.

D. Grammar. Complete the sentences. Write <u>am</u>, <u>is</u>, or <u>are</u>.

1. I _____ from Florida.   2. He _____ a plumber.

3. She _____ not a manager.   4. You _____ my partner.

➤ Do it yourself!

1. Point. Say the occupations.
   A bus driver

2. Point. Ask questions.
   Is he a student?

3. Create conversations for the people.
   A: What do you do?
   B: I'm a cashier.

4. Say more about the picture. Use your <u>own</u> words. Say as much as you can.

Now I can talk about
❑ names.
❑ occupations.
❑ where I am from.
❑ _____.

The community

> **Vocabulary**

Objectives
- talk about places
- ask for directions
- give directions

Picture dictionary

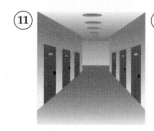    

🎧 **A.** Listen.

Workplaces		**Rooms and other places**		**Other words**
① a hospital	⑤ a restaurant	⑧ a restroom	⑫ an office	⑮ a person
② a post office	⑥ a supermarket	⑨ a supply room	⑬ an exit	⑯ people
③ a bank	⑦ a parking lot	⑩ a meeting room	⑭ an entrance	⑰ old
④ a school		⑪ a hall		⑱ new

🎧 **B.** Listen again and repeat.

🎧 **C.** Now listen and point to the pictures.

🎧 **How to say it**

at home

at work

at school

at 22 Church Street

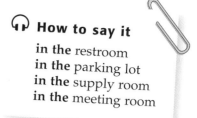

🎧 **How to say it**

in the restroom
in the parking lot
in the supply room
in the meeting room

D. Write the name of each place. Write <u>a</u> or <u>an</u>.

1. _a meeting room_

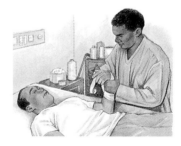

2. _____

3. _____

4. _____

5. _____

6. _____

➤ Do it yourself!

A. Write the names of other rooms or places. Write <u>a</u> or <u>an</u>.

1. _a kitchen_

2. _____

3. _____

4. _____

B. Pair work. Read your words to your partner.

Unit 2   25

Practical conversations

Model 1 Ask about people.

⌒ **A. Listen and read.**

A: Are Sandra and Elena here?
B: No, they're not. They're in the office.
A: Excuse me?
B: They're in the office.

⌒ **B. Listen again and repeat.**

C. Pair work. Now ask about real people.

A: Are _____ and _____ here?
B: No, they're not. They're _____.
A: Excuse me?
B: They're _____.

Model 2 Ask about places.

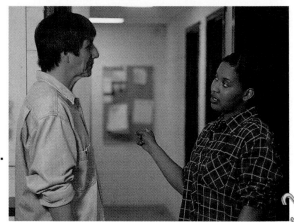

⌒ **A. Listen and read.**

A: Where are the restrooms?
B: They're down the hall, on the right.

⌒ **B. Listen again and repeat.**

C. Pair work. Now ask about places on the map.

A: Where are the _____s?
B: They're down the hall, on _____.

Left and Right

Left   **Right**
◀   ▶

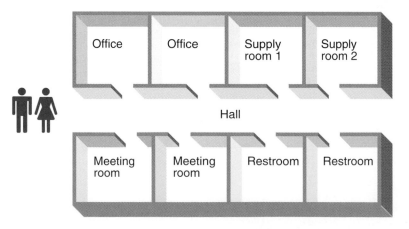

| Office | Office | Supply room 1 | Supply room 2 |

Hall

| Meeting room | Meeting room | Restroom | Restroom |

A. Listen and read.

A: Excuse me. I'm looking for the post office.

B: The post office? It's on Main Street. It's next to the bank.

A: Thanks.

B: You're welcome.

B. Listen again and repeat.

C. Pair work. Now talk about places on the map.

A: Excuse me. I'm looking for the _____.

B: The _____? It's _____.

A: _____.

B: You're welcome.

How to say it

Main Street

It's **on** Main Street.

bank

It's **across from** the bank.

bank   school

It's **between** the bank **and** the school.

bank

It's **next to** the bank.

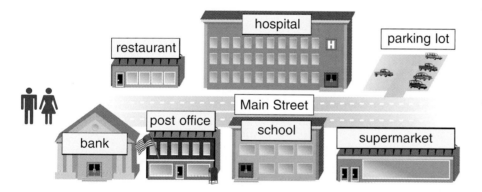

➤ Do it yourself!

Pair work. **Create a conversation from the picture. Ask for directions. Give directions.**

Practical grammar

Be: plural

We			We		
You	**are** in the supply room.		You	**are not** in the office.	
They			They		

🎧 **Contractions**

we
you + are = we're
they   you're
                 they're

we are + not = we're not

A. Complete the conversations. Write <u>We're</u>, <u>They're</u>, or <u>they're</u>.

1. **A:** Are Sandra and Elena here?

   B: No, they're not. _____ in the office.

2. **A:** Are we in Meeting Room A?

   B: No, we're not. _____ in Meeting Room B.

3. **A:** Where are they? In the parking lot?

   B: No, _____ not in the parking lot. They're in the supply room.

4. **A:** Are the offices down the hall?

   B: No, _____ across from the meeting room.

Are we				we				we're	
Are you	partners?		Yes,	you	**are**.		No,	you're	**not**.
Are they				they				they're	

B. Complete the conversations. Write the words on the line.

1. **A:** Are they in the supply room?

   B: No, _____ not.

2. **A:** Allen and Eva, _____ engineers?

   B: Yes, we are.

3. **A:** _____ here?

   B: Yes, but they're in the restroom right now.

Where's the post office?	It's on Main Street.
What's your occupation?	I'm a cashier in the new restaurant.
Who are they?	Mary and Carmen.

C. Complete the questions. Choose words. Write the words on the line.

1. _Where_ are Luis and Paco?   In the parking lot.
   What / Where

2. _____ your address?   It's 10 Main Street.
   What's / Who's

3. Excuse me. _____ the bank?   It's on Water Street.
   Who's / Where's

4. _____ in the parking lot?   Donna.
   Who's / What's

5. _____ are you from?   Guatemala.
   What / Where

➤ Do it yourself!

A. Ask questions about the picture. Use Where, Who, and What.

A: Where's the restaurant?
B: It's next to the school.

B. Personalization. Now tell your partner about a place in your neighborhood.

The bank is between the supermarket and the parking lot.

With words you know, (YOU) can talk to this man.

🎧 **A.** Listen and read.

Man: May I help you?

YOU *Yes. I'm looking for Manuel's Restaurant.*

Man: Manuel's? It's right around the corner. On Hill Street. Do you know where that is?

YOU *Hill Street? Yes.*

Man: Well, Manuel's is down that street . . . in the new building next to the parking lot. It's on the right-hand side of the street.

YOU *Excuse me?*

Man: It's on Hill Street. On the right. Next to the parking lot.

YOU *Thanks.*

Man: Sure. No problem.

🎧 **B.** Listen to the man. Read **your** part.

🎧 **C.** Listen and read. Choose **your** response. Circle the letter.

1. "Do you know where the parking lot is?"

   a. Oh, yes. It's next to Green's Supermarket. **b.** Thanks.

2. "It's on the right side of the street."

   a. Well, good luck!   **b.** Next to the post office?

3. "It's right around the corner."

   a. I'm looking for the school.   **b.** On Lake Street?

🎧 **D.** Listen. Choose **your** response. Circle the letter.

1. **a.** Thank you very much.   **b.** Excuse me?

2. **a.** Next to the parking lot? Good.   **b.** Oh, yes.

3. **a.** Yes. I'm looking for the bank.   **b.** Yes. Excuse me.

🎧 **Listen to the conversations. Then listen again. Write the place on the map.**

1. Where's the supply room?

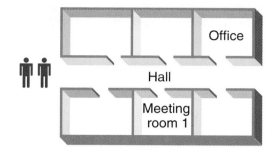

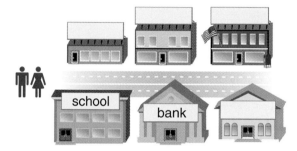

2. Where's the supermarket?

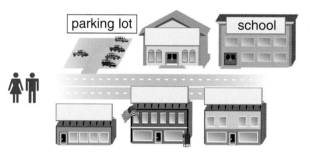

3. Where's the hospital?

➤ Do it yourself!

A. Use the map from question 3. Write your <u>own</u> response. Then read your conversation out loud with a partner.

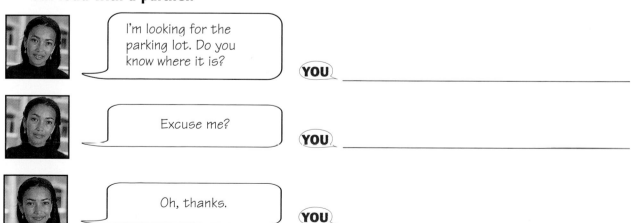

I'm looking for the parking lot. Do you know where it is?

YOU _____

Excuse me?

YOU _____

Oh, thanks.

YOU _____

B. Discussion. Talk about places at work or in the neighborhood.

Authentic practice 2

Reading

A. Look at the poster. Circle the occupations.

HELP WANTED

Get a good job at **CENTRAL HOSPITAL!**

NOW HIRING:

- Housekeepers
- Cooks
- Pharmacist Assistants
- Cashiers
- Office Managers
- Plumbers
- Ambulance Drivers
- Bus Drivers
- Respiratory Therapists
- Nurse's Aides

**Open interviews
Saturday, November 12
9 a.m. to 5 p.m.**

Central Hospital
1200 West Street
Dallas, Texas 79702
(217) 555-7524

The hospital is across from the Bank of Texas.
Park in the lot next to the bank.

B. Now read the poster. Check ☑ yes or no.

	yes	no
1. The name of the workplace is Central Hospital.	☐	☐
2. It's on Dallas Street.	☐	☐
3. The zip code is 75240.	☐	☐
4. Central Hospital is looking for office managers.	☐	☐
5. The hospital is next to the Bank of Texas.	☐	☐

C. Critical thinking. **Can they get jobs at Central Hospital? Write yes or no.**

1. Mia Kim is a bus driver. __yes__

2. Todd Williams is a restaurant manager. _____

3. Hillary Dennis is a cook. _____

4. Sandra Morin is a teacher. _____

5. Kevin Chung is a mechanic. _____

A. Make a map of a workplace. Write the rooms and other places on your map. Use words from the box.

| supply room | restrooms | entrance | office | meeting room |

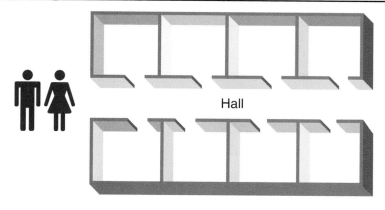

Hall

B. Complete these notes about your map.

I'm in the office right now. It's

_____

_____.

Hi:
The books are in the supply room.
The supply room is _____

_____.

C. Discussion. Compare your map and notes with your partner's map and notes.

> **Do it yourself!** A class project

A. Collaborative activity.
Write a list of places in the neighborhood. Then make a map on the chalkboard.

B. Discussion.
Talk about the map.

▶ Review

A. Vocabulary. Look at the pictures. Write places from the box. Write **a** or **an**.

post office	supply room	office	parking lot

1. _____

2. _____

3. _____

4. _____

B. Vocabulary. Complete the sentences.

1. The bank is _____ the post office.

2. The hospital is _____ the parking lot.

C. Conversation. Choose **your** response. Circle the letter.

1. "Are Petra and Evan here?"

   a. No, they're at work.   **b.** They're Petra and Evan.

2. "Excuse me. I'm looking for the old school."

   a. Where is the school?   **b.** It's across from the parking lot.

3. "Thanks."

   a. No problem.   **b.** It's down the hall.

D. Grammar. Complete the sentences. Write **is**, **Are**, or **'re not**.

1. **A:** Where _____ the hospital?

   B: The hospital _____ next to the bank.

2. **A:** _____ you in Meeting Room 1?

   B: No, we_____.

E. Writing. Answer the questions.

1. Where is the supermarket?   _On Main Street. Next to the bank._

2. Where is **your** supermarket? _____

3. Where is **your** school? _____

➤ Do it yourself!

1. Point. Name the places.
   A bank

2. Point. Talk about the people.
   They're students.

3. Create conversations for the people.
   A: *Excuse me. Where's the post office?*
   B: *It's across from the restaurant.*

4. Say more about the picture. Use your <u>own</u> words. Say as much as you can.

Now I can
❑ talk about places.
❑ ask for directions.
❑ give directions.

❑ _____.

Technology

Vocabulary

Picture dictionary

🎧 **A.** Listen.

Machines		**Parts of machines**	**Actions**	
① a copier	⑤ a coffee maker	⑧ a button	⑬ open	⑰ unplug
② a computer	⑥ a lawn mower	⑨ a key	⑭ close	⑱ call
③ a telephone	⑦ a cash register	⑩ a door	⑮ press	
④ a microwave		⑪ a lid	⑯ turn	
		⑫ directions		

🎧 **B.** Listen again and repeat.

🎧 **C.** Now listen and point to the pictures.

🎧 **How to say it**

off   on

D. **Match the pictures and the sentences. Write the letter on the line.**

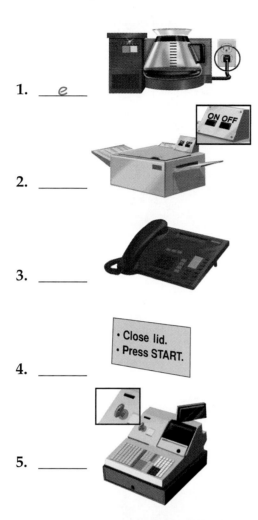

1. __e__

2. _____

3. _____

4. _____

5. _____

a. Read the directions.

b. Call Mr. Ruvo, please.
His number is 555–2144.

c. Turn the key.

d. Press the button.

e. Unplug the machine, please.

➤ Do it yourself!

A. **Collaborative activity. Complete the chart. Use machines from page 36. Or use your own machines. Write a or an.**

a button	a key	a lid or door
a copier		

B. **Read your chart to your class.**

Model 1   Make a suggestion. Get help.

 A. Listen and read.

    A: Oh, no!

    B: What's wrong?

    A: The cash register is out of order.

    B: Let's call Ms. Rivas.

    A: Good idea.

B. Listen again and repeat.

C. Pair work. Now use your own words.

    A: Oh, no!

    B: What's wrong?

    A: The _____ is out of order.

    B: Let's call _____.

    A: Good idea.

Models 2 and 3   Give directions. Give a warning.

A. Listen and read.

    A: Press the <u>on</u> button.

    B: OK.

    A: Don't press the <u>off</u> button.

    B: No problem.

B. Listen again and repeat.

How to say it

Don't open the door!

C. Pair work. Now use the pictures. Or talk about your own machine.

    A: _____ the _____.

    B: _____.

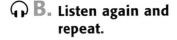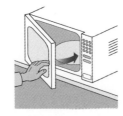

A. Listen and read.

A: How do I start the coffee maker?
B: Press the <u>on</u> button.
A: OK. And how do I start the microwave?
B: I don't know.

B. Listen again and repeat.

C. Pair work. Now use the pictures or your <u>own</u> machines.

A: How do I start the _____?
B: _____.
A: OK. And how do I start the _____?
B: I don't know.

➤ Do it yourself!

Pair work. **Create a conversation for the people about machines. Use your <u>own</u> words.**

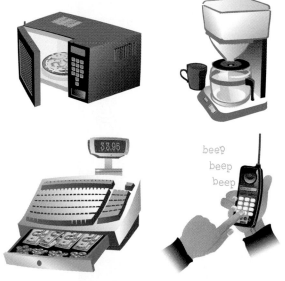

beep
beep
beep

Suggestions with Let's

Let's start the coffee maker.

Let's read. Good idea.

A. Complete the suggestions. Use **Let's**.

1. **A:** Oh, no!
    B: What's wrong?
    A: The new cash register's out of order.
    B: _____ John.
    A: OK. What's the number?

2. **A:** _____ the computer.
    B: OK. Press the <u>on</u> button.

3. **A:** How do I start the copier?
    B: I don't know. _____ the directions.
    A: Good idea.

B. Write suggestions with **Let's**. Use the words in the box.

call the manager	close the door	~~start the computer~~	open the door

1. _Let's start the computer._ _____

2. _____

3. _____

4. _____

Press the <u>on</u> button.　　**Turn** the key, please.

C. **Complete the sentences. Write the words from the box.**

Call	open	~~Press~~	Turn

1. Start the coffee maker. _Press_ the <u>on</u> button.

2. Let's start the lawn mower. _____ the key.

3. _____ the manager. The phone number is 555–4801.

4. Please _____ the lid of the copier.

Negative commands

Don't press the <u>off</u> button.　　**Don't unplug** the computer, please.

D. **Write negative commands. Choose a verb. Use <u>Don't</u>.**

1. _Don't start_ the lawn mower.
   start / open

2. _____ the copier, please.
   call / unplug

3. Please _____ the coffee maker.
   start / close

4. _____ the <u>on</u> button.
   start / press

5. _____ the door of the microwave.
   open / start

> ➤ **Do it yourself!**

Give directions to the office workers.

Unplug the coffee maker.

COFFEE MAKER
DIRECTIONS
• Add water.
• Add coffee.
• Press ON.
IF BROKEN
CALL 553-7643

ON
OFF

Authentic practice 1

With words you know, YOU can talk to this co-worker.

🎧 **A.** Listen and read.

Co-worker: Oh, no. What's the problem?

YOU *The machine is out of order.*

Co-worker: Again? What's wrong with it?

YOU *I don't know.*

Co-worker: Well, maybe we need to call the manager.

YOU *OK. Good idea. What's the number?*

Co-worker: It's extension 3023, I think.

YOU *Thanks.*

🎧 **B.** Listen to the co-worker. Read <u>your</u> part.

🎧 **C.** Listen and read. Choose <u>your</u> response. Circle the letter.

1. "What's wrong?"
   a. The cash register is out of order. **b.** It's OK.

2. "Did you turn the key?"
   a. Good luck. **b.** Yes.

3. "Maybe we need to call the manager."
   a. OK. What's the number? **b.** No, it's not.

🎧 **D.** Listen. Choose <u>your</u> response. Circle the letter.

1. **a.** Good idea. **b.** It's out of order.

2. **a.** 575–1222. **b.** Mr. Harris.

3. **a.** Oh, yes. **b.** What's wrong?

🎧 **A.** Listen to the conversations. Then read the sentences. Write <u>yes</u> or <u>no</u>.

1. The conversations are about directions for machines. _____

2. The machines are out of order. _____

🎧 **B.** Listen again. Read the directions for each machine. Circle the letter.

1.
    a. Press <u>on</u>.
    b. Press the <u>off</u> button.

2.
    a. Turn the key to the right.
    b. Turn the key to the left.

3.
    a. Close the door and press <u>start</u>.
    b. Unplug the microwave.

➤ Do it yourself!

A. Write your <u>own</u> response. Then read your conversation out loud with a partner.

 What's the problem with the machine?

YOU _____

 Is it on or off?

YOU _____

 Well, if it's really out of order, let's call the manager.

YOU _____

B. Discussion. Talk about machines at home or at work.

Authentic practice 2

A. Look at the card. Then write <u>yes</u> or <u>no</u>.

WORLDWIDE
TELEPHONE COMPANY

INSTRUCTIONS

1. Call 1-800-555-0237.
2. Press the card number.
3. Press 1, the area code, and the number you want to call. (For international calls, press 011, the country code, and the number.)

▶ | 182-508-0510 |
Card number

Prepaid Phone Card
30 minutes

1. The card is for telephone calls.

_____

2. The card gives directions.

_____

B. Critical thinking. Read the Worldwide Telephone Company card. Then write the directions to call the Good Morning Restaurant.

(973) 555-5101

GOOD MORNING
R E S T A U R A N T

Breakfast and lunch

2054 Park Street
Chicago, IL
(973) 555-3000

Call for
the res
downto
Reserva

Open for
Please c

1. Call _____.

2. Then press _____.

3. Then press _____.

**Look at the pictures and the directions. Complete the directions.
Write words from the box.**

card	directions	Press	Press	put	~~telephone~~

Coin calls

Card calls

911 calls are free.

INSTRUCTIONS

Put 25 cents in the ___telephone___. _____ the
    1.   2.

telephone number.

Call the 800 number on the telephone _____.
                                          3.

Follow the _____ on the telephone card.
                  4.

_____ 911. Don't _____ 25 cents in the
      5.   6.

telephone.

➤**Do it yourself!**   A plan-ahead project

A. Discussion. **Bring a phone card to class or use the
card here. Talk about the directions on the card.**

> Press 1, the area code,
> and the phone number.

B. Pair work. **Give your partner directions
to make a phone call with the card.**

Telephone Company

Instructions:

1. Call 1-800-555-8900.
2. Press 1, the area code, and the telephone number.
3. Press the calling card number. ▼

345–549–8222
Card number

Prepaid
Telephone
Calling Card

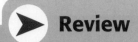

A. Vocabulary. Write the names of the machines. Write <u>a</u> or <u>an</u>.

1. _____

2. _____

3. _____

4. _____

B. Conversation. Choose <u>your</u> response. Circle the letter.

1. "Don't open the door."

   a. OK. No problem.   **b.** I don't know.

2. "Let's unplug the computer."

   a. OK.   **b.** How do I start the computer?

3. "How do I start the computer?"

   a. I don't know.   **b.** Good idea.

C. Grammar. Write suggestions with <u>Let's</u>. Use the verbs from the box.

~~call~~	read	press

1.  *Let's call the manager.* _____

2. _____

3.  Directions
Close the lid.
Press START. _____

D. Reading and writing. Complete the directions.

1. _____ the door.

2. _____ the <u>start</u> button.

3. _____ the <u>stop</u> button.

4. _____ the door.

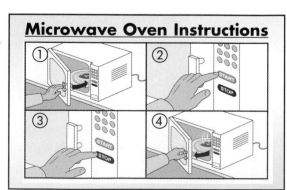

Microwave Oven Instructions

① ② ③ ④

➤ Do it yourself!

1. Point. Name the machines.

   A copier

2. What's wrong? Tell your partner.

   The coffee maker is out of order.

3. Create conversations for the people.

   A: Press the off button.
   B: OK.

4. Say more about the picture. Use your own words. Say as much as you can.

Now I can
❑ talk about machines.
❑ understand and give directions for machines.
❑ make suggestions.
❑ _____.

The consumer world

Vocabulary

Objectives

Talk about
- colors and sizes
- problems with clothes
- likes and dislikes
- refunds and exchanges

Picture dictionary

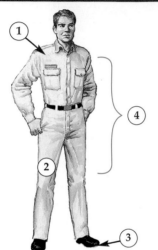

🎧 **A.** Listen.

Clothes		Colors		Other words
① a shirt	⑥ a tie	⑩ red	⑭ black	⑱ a customer
② pants	⑦ a dress	⑪ blue	⑮ green	⑲ a salesperson
③ a shoe	⑧ a skirt	⑫ yellow	⑯ orange	⑳ a receipt
④ a uniform	⑨ a jacket	⑬ white	⑰ brown	㉑ a store
⑤ a suit				

🎧 **B.** Listen again and repeat.

🎧 **C.** Now listen and point to the pictures.

D. Match the pictures and the words. Write the letter on the line.

1. ___e___

2. _____

3. _____

4. _____

5. _____

6. _____

    a. a green dress

    b. an orange shirt

    c. a blue shirt

    d. an orange tie

    e. a green uniform

    f. a blue uniform

➤ Do it yourself!

A. Write about three classmates and their clothes.

Hi, I'm Tim.

Name	Clothes
Tim	black shoes, a white shirt, blue pants, an orange tie
1.	
2.	
3.	

B. Pair work. Read your list of clothes. Your partner guesses the names.

Practical conversations

Model 1　Ask for service. Offer service.

🎧 **A.** **Listen and read.**

    A: I need a uniform, please.
    B: Sure. What size?
    A: Small.
    B: And what color?
    A: Green.
    B: OK. This way, please.

🎧 **B.** **Listen again and repeat.**

C. Pair work. **Now use your <u>own</u> words.**

    A: I need _____, please.
    B: _____. What size?
    A: _____.
    B: And what color?
    A: _____.
    B: _____. This way, please.

🎧 **Sizes**

small   medium   large

Model 2　Ask for a size.

🎧 **A.** **Listen and read.**

    A: Do you have this shirt in large?
    B: Yes, we do.
    A: Do you have these shoes in size 10?
    B: No, we don't. I'm sorry.

🎧 **B.** **Listen again and repeat.**

C. Pair work. **Now use the pictures.**

    A: Do you have this _____ in _____?
    B: Yes, _____.

    A: Do you have these _____ in _____?
    B: No, _____. I'm sorry.

this   these

A. Listen and read.

> A: May I help you?
> B: Yes, please. These pants are the wrong size.
> A: Oh, I'm sorry. Do you have the receipt?
> B: Yes, I think so.

B. Listen again and repeat.

C. Pair work. Now use your own problems.

> A: May I help you?
> B: Yes, please. These pants are _____.
> A: Oh, I'm sorry. Do you have the receipt?
> B: Yes, I think so.

Problems with clothes

the wrong size
the wrong color
too small
too large

➤ Do it yourself!

Pair work. Create a conversation from the pictures. Use your own words.

Practical grammar

The simple present tense: <u>have</u>, <u>want</u>, <u>need</u>, and <u>like</u>

I
You
We
They } **need** a uniform.

I
You
We
They } **don't need** a tie.

She **wants** the shirt.

He **needs** a book.

She **likes** red shoes.

Now he **has** a book.

She **doesn't need** a shirt. He **doesn't want** a new tie.

A. **Complete each sentence with the simple present tense. Write the verb on the line.**

1. I _____ a uniform, please.
   <u>need / needs</u>

2. We _____ that T-shirt in small.
   <u>have / has</u>

3. Marisol _____ black shoes.
   <u>want / wants</u>

4. I _____ this suit. It's too large.
   <u>don't like / doesn't like</u>

Questions and short answers

Do { you
they } like this tie?   Yes, { I
we
they } do.   No, { I
we
they } don't.

Does { he
she
Bill } like this tie?   Yes, { he
she
Bill } does.   No, { he
she
Bill } doesn't.

Information questions

What size do { you
they } want?

B. **Answer each question with a short answer.**

1. Do you like green shoes? Yes, _____.

2. Do they have uniforms? Yes, _____.

3. Does Carlos need a tie? No, _____.

4. Does he want a blue suit? Yes, _____.

C. **Complete the questions. Choose words. Write the words on the line.**

1. _____ you _____ this new tie?
   <u>Do / Does</u>   <u>want / wants</u>

2. _____ she _____ a black skirt?
   <u>Do / Does</u>   <u>have / has</u>

3. What _____ they _____?
   <u>do / does</u>   <u>like / likes</u>

This, that, these, those

I like **this** suit.

I like **that** suit.

I like **these** shoes.

I like **those** shoes.

D. **Look at the pictures. Complete the sentences. Use <u>this</u>, <u>that</u>, <u>these</u>, or <u>those</u>.**

1. I like __*this*__ uniform.

2. Please press _____ button.

3. We don't need more blue pants. We have _____ blue pants.

4. I want _____ shoes.

➤ Do it yourself!

A. **Pair work. Point. Ask and answer questions about the people.**

A: *Does she want the red dress?*
B: *No. She wants the black dress.*

B. **Personalization. Look at the picture. What do <u>you</u> like? Tell your partner.**

I like the computer.

C. **Tell the class about your partner.**

My partner likes the red dress.

With words you know, YOU can talk to this customer.

🎧 **A.** Listen and read.

Customer: Hi, I need some help. I need to return this microwave oven. It's too large.

YOU *I'm sorry. . . . Well, no problem. Do you have the receipt?*

Customer: Yes, I do. Here it is. Do you have any small microwaves?

YOU *Yes, I think so.*

Customer: Oh, that's good. Where are they?

YOU *They're across from the coffee makers.*

Customer: Great, thanks.

🎧 **B.** Listen to the customer. Read <u>your</u> part.

🎧 **C.** Listen and read. Choose <u>your</u> response. Circle the letter.

1. "Hi, I need some help."

   a. It's too large.   **b.** Sure.

2. "These shirts are the wrong color."

   a. Oh, I'm sorry.   **b.** That's good.

3. "Where are the computers?"

   a. This way, please.   **b.** They're from Japan.

🎧 **D.** Listen. Choose <u>your</u> response. Circle the letter.

1. **a.** Great, thanks.   **b.** Sure, what size?

2. **a.** Yes, please.   **b.** Do you have the receipt?

3. **a.** OK. Are they too small?   **b.** You're welcome.

A. Listen to the conversation. Read the form. Then circle the answer to the question.

Peerless Uniform Company   ORDER FORM

Customer's Name: ___Oscar Soto___

Uniform: ☐ housekeeper   ☑ nurse   ☐ cook   ☐ bus driver

Color: ☑ green ☐ blue ☐ white ☐ black ☐ red ☐ yellow ☐ orange ☐ brown

Size:	small	medium	large	extra large
Shirt	☐	☐	☑	☐
Pants	☐	☑	☐	☐
Skirt	☐	☐	☐	☐

Who is talking to Mr. Soto?   **a.** a customer   **b.** a salesperson

B. Listen to the conversation. Then listen again and complete the order form.

Peerless Uniform Company   ORDER FORM

Customer's Name: ___Martin Yu___

Uniform: ☐ housekeeper   ☐ nurse   ☐ cook   ☐ bus driver

Color: ☐ green ☐ blue ☐ white ☐ black ☐ red ☐ yellow ☐ orange ☐ brown

Size:	small	medium	large	extra large
Shirt	☐	☐	☐	☐
Pants	☐	☐	☐	☐
Skirt	☐	☐	☐	☐

➤ Do it yourself!

A. Write your <u>own</u> response. Then read your conversation out loud with a partner.

I have a problem. These pants are too small.

(YOU) _____

Here's my receipt.

(YOU) _____

I need some shoes. Could you please tell me where they are?

(YOU) _____

B. Discussion. Talk about a problem with clothes.

Reading

A. Read the sign.

Bell Office Supply

REFUND AND EXCHANGE POLICY

No refunds.
Exchanges for customers
with receipts.

🎧 **Refunds and exchanges**

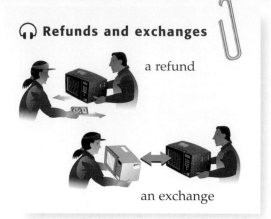

a refund

an exchange

B. Critical thinking. Read about these customers at Bell Office Supply. Choose a response for each customer.

No problem.

We don't give refunds. I'm sorry.

I'm sorry. You need a receipt.

Tanaka

1. Ella Tanaka wants a refund for a copier. She has the receipt.

Response: <u>We don't give refunds. I'm sorry.</u>

Gonzales

2. Pedro Gonzales wants to exchange copier paper. It's the wrong size. He has the receipt.

Response: _____

Martinez

3. Alice Martinez wants to exchange a computer. She doesn't need the computer. She doesn't have the receipt.

Response: _____

Gammon

4. John Gammon wants a refund for a coffee maker. He doesn't like the coffee maker. He has the receipt.

Response: _____

A. Look at the return form. Then answer the questions.

> **Bell Office Supply** | **Exchange Department**
>
> Customer name: _____ *Pedro Gonzales* _____
>
> Item: _____ *copier paper* _____
>
> Reason for return: _____ *wrong size* _____

1. What's the customer's name? _____

2. What does the customer want to return? _____

3. What's the problem? _____

B. Gregory Lin wants to exchange a red telephone. He wants a black telephone. Complete the return form for Mr. Lin.

> **Bell Office Supply** | **Exchange Department**
>
> Customer name: _____
>
> Item: _____
>
> Reason for return: _____

➤ Do it yourself!   A plan-ahead project

Discussion. Bring receipts to class. Compare your receipts. Or use these receipts.

What's the name of the store?

Does the store give refunds?

Clothes & More

Date Sept. 18/02

Name			
Address			Check
Salesperson Carol	Cash X	Charge	Amount
Quantity	Item		
1	Walking shorts - blue		29.95
1	T-shirt, crew neck - white		12.00
1	T-shirt, crew neck - black		12.00
			53.95
All claims and returned goods MUST be accompanied by this bill.		TAX	2.26
Return Policy: STORE CREDIT OR EXCHANGE ONLY. NO CASH OR CREDIT CARD REFUNDS.		TOTAL	$56.21

Ann's Closet

Sold to

Address

Sold By Tom C	Cash ✓	C.O.D.	Charge	On Acct.	Mdse. Ret'd.	Paid Out
Qty.	Description				Price	Amount
1	Shirt					17.95
1	Jacket					22.95
	10% off					-4.09

FINAL SALE NO REFUNDS. EXCHANGE ONLY WITH RECEIPT.

| | | Tax | 1.53 |
| | | Total | $38.34 |

Review

A. Vocabulary. Match the picture with the words. Write the letter on the line.

1. _____ old shoes

2. _____ a yellow uniform

3. _____ an old T-shirt

4. _____ a yellow skirt

a.

b.

c.

d.

B. Conversation. Choose <u>your</u> response. Circle the letter.

1. "I need a white shirt."

   a. OK. This way, please.   **b.** What color, please?

2. "Do you have these shoes in brown?"

   a. May I help you?   **b.** No, I'm sorry.

3. "These pants are the wrong size."

   a. Oh, I'm sorry.   **b.** Yes, we do.

C. Grammar. Choose the verb. Write the verb on the line.

1. Maria _____ large T-shirts.

like / likes

2. Ed _____ an old computer.

have / has

3. We _____ a new copier for the meeting room.

want / wants

4. The cashier _____ the key for the cash register.

doesn't have / don't have

D. Writing. Return a coffee maker to Best Appliances. It's the wrong color. Complete the form.

BEST APPLIANCES

Customer Service: Returns

Name: _____

Address: _____

Item you wish to return: _____

Reason for return: _____

➤ Do it yourself!

1. Point. Name the clothes.

A yellow shirt

2. Point. Ask questions.

Do the students like those shirts?

3. Create conversations for the people.

A: May I help you?
B: Yes. This coffee maker is too small.

4. Say more about the picture. Use your <u>own</u> words. Say as much as you can.

Now I can talk about
❑ colors and sizes.
❑ problems with clothes.
❑ likes and dislikes.
❑ refunds and exchanges.
❑ _____.

Time

Vocabulary

Picture dictionary

(1)

(2)

(3)

(4)

(5)

(6) 2001 January S M T W T F S

(7) 2001 January S M T W T F S

(8) 2001 January S M T W T F S

(9) **Today is June 6, 2001**

(10) **June 7, 2001**

A. Listen.

The time	(6) Months of the year		(7) Days of the week		Other words
(1) 8:00 = eight o'clock	January	July	Sunday	Thursday	(8) a year
(2) 10:05 = ten-oh-five	February	August	Monday	Friday	(9) today
(3) 2:15 = two fifteen	March	September	Tuesday	Saturday	(10) tomorrow
(4) 11:30 = eleven thirty	April	October	Wednesday		
(5) 6:45 = six forty-five	May	November			
	June	December			

B. Listen again and repeat.

C. Now listen and point to the pictures.

D. Match the clocks and the times. Write the letter on the line.

1. ___b___

2. _____

3. _____

4. _____

5. _____

a. 12:00

b. 8:55

c. 4:15

d. 9:30

e. 11:45

E. Read the time card and the receipt. Then answer the questions.

TIME CARD

		IN	OUT
Tuesday	July 17, 2001	2:30	

```
*************************************
        BEST SUPERMARKET
*************************************
Friday, August 9, 2002        7:15

Potatoes                     $1.99
Cheese                       $2.99
```

1. What day is it?   _Tuesday_
2. What month is it?   _____
3. What year is it?   _____
4. What time is it?   _____

1. What day is it?   _____
2. What month is it?   _____
3. What year is it?   _____
4. What time is it?   _____

What day is today?

> **Do it yourself!**

Sunday.

A. Answer the questions.

1. What day is today?   _____
2. What day is tomorrow?   _____
3. What month is it?   _____
4. What time is it right now? _____

B. Pair work. Check answers with your partner.

Practical conversations

Model 1   What time is it?

A. Listen and read.

A: What time is it?
B: It's 3:15.
A: 3:15? Uh-oh. I'm late. Bye.
B: Bye. See you later.

B. Listen again and repeat.

C. Pair work. Now use real times.

A: What time is it?
B: It's _____.
A: _____? Uh-oh. I'm late. Bye.
B: _____.

More times

9:00 a.m.   9:00 p.m.   noon   midnight

Model 2   Ask about schedules.

A. Listen and read.

A: When does school start?
B: In September.
A: And when does it end?
B: In June.

B. Listen again and repeat.

C. Pair work. Now ask about school and work.

A: When does _____ start?
B: _____.
A: And when does it end?
B: _____.

How to say it

in September
on Wednesday
at 3:00
today
tomorrow

A. Listen and read.

A: What time does the post office open?
B: At 8:30 a.m.
A: And when does it close?
B: I'm not sure. At noon, I think.
A: At noon? That's great!

B. Listen again and repeat.

C. Pair work. Now look at the signs. Talk about the places.

A: What time does _____?
B: _____.
A: And when does it _____?
B: _____, I think.
A: At _____? That's great!

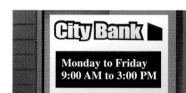

➤ Do it yourself!

A. Personalization. Choose places in your neighborhood. Complete the signs for the places. Write opening and closing times.

B. Discussion. Talk about the places in your neighborhood.

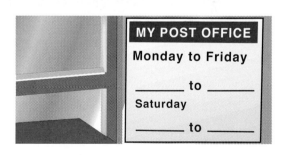

Practical grammar

It's for days, dates, and times

It's Sunday.
It's 2002.
It's midnight.
It's 5:10.
Is it 4:15?   Yes, it is. / No, it isn't.

A. Choose words. Write the words on the line.

1. What day is it? ___It's___ Monday.

Is / It's

2. What time is it? _____ 5:20.

Is / It's

3. _____ April 15 or April 16?   Neither! It's April 17!

It is / Is it

Questions with What time and When

What time does work start?	At 9:00.
When is the bank open?	From Monday to Friday.
When is the class?	At 6:50.

B. Write a question with **What time is** or **What time does**.

1. **A:** _What time does the supermarket open?_ _____

   B: The supermarket opens at 7:30.

2. **A:** _____?

   B: It's 1:30.

C. Write a question with **When is** or **When does**.

1. **A:** _____?

   B: The restaurant closes at 11:00 p.m.

2. **A:** _____?

   B: The class is at 3:15.

Ordinal numbers from 1 to 31

Write the date with a number.

March **5**, 2000.
June **1**, 2003.

Say the date with an ordinal number.

"It's March **fifth**."
"It's June **first**."

Ordinal numbers

first	ninth	seventeenth
second	tenth	eighteenth
third	eleventh	nineteenth
fourth	twelfth	twentieth
fifth	thirteenth	twenty-first
sixth	fourteenth	twenty-second
seventh	fifteenth	thirtieth
eighth	sixteenth	thirty-first

🎧 **D. Read and listen to the ordinal numbers in the box. Then listen again and repeat.**

🎧 **E. Listen to the conversations. Then complete the dates.**

1. March __1__
2. October _____
3. April _____
4. August _____

Say the dates out loud to a partner.

➤ Do it yourself!

A. Pair work. Ask questions about the picture. Use What time and When.

A: What time does the bank open?
B: 9:00.

B. Personalization. Now talk to your partner about your supermarket.

My supermarket opens at 8:30 a.m.

With words you know, YOU can talk to this manager.

🎧 **A. Listen and read.**

Manager: Good morning. Oh, it's 9:00.
You're right on time. That's great.

YOU *Thank you.*

Manager: Well, let me tell you a little about the job.
Your shift starts at 6:00.

YOU *6:00 a.m.?*

Manager: Well, actually no. At 6:00 p.m.

YOU *Good. No problem.*

Manager: Can you start this Tuesday, March 5?

YOU *I think so. . . . Yes, that's OK.*

Manager: Terrific! See you on Tuesday. Please be a
little early on your first day.

YOU *Sure. What time?*

Manager: How about 5:45?

YOU *OK.*

🎧 **B. Listen to the manager. Read <u>your</u> part.**

🎧 **C. Listen and read. Choose <u>your</u> response. Circle the letter.**

1. "You're a little early. That's good."

   a. Thanks.   **b.** I'm sorry.

2. "Let me tell you a little about the job. Your shift starts at 6:00."

   a. I think so.   **b.** That's OK.

3. "Can you start on Tuesday, March 5?"

   a. No problem.   **b.** Press <u>start</u>.

🎧 **D. Listen. Choose <u>your</u> response. Circle the letter.**

1. **a.** Sure. What time does work start?   **b.** That's great.

2. **a.** Uh oh. I'm late.   **b.** Yes, sure.

3. **a.** OK.   **b.** I don't know.

🎧 **A. Listen to the conversation. Then complete each sentence. Circle the letter.**

1. The people are talking about _____.

   a. time and dates

   b. clothes and sizes

   c. buildings and places

2. The people are _____.

   a. a manager and a new employee

   b. a customer and a salesperson

   c. a student and a teacher

🎧 **B. Listen to the conversation again. Circle Mr. Oakdale's start date and start time.**

Start date	Start time
May 18	8:15
May 8	8:50

➤ **Do it yourself!**

A. Write your <u>own</u> response. Then read your conversation out loud with a partner.

Can you start tomorrow on the 11:00 p.m. shift? **YOU** _____

On Mondays you need to be a little early. Is that OK for you? **YOU** _____

OK. See you this Monday at 10:00. **YOU** _____

B. Discussion. Talk about the time work or school starts.

Authentic practice 2

Reading

**A. Critical thinking. Look at the work schedule and time card.
Is Claire Costello early, on time, or late?**

WORK SCHEDULE	WEEK OF *January 24*
MONDAY	*3:00 p.m.–9:00 p.m.*
TUESDAY	*7:00 a.m.–3:00 p.m.*
WEDNESDAY	*6:00 a.m.–2:00 p.m.*
THURSDAY	*3:00 p.m.–9:00 p.m.*
FRIDAY	*6:00 a.m.–12:00 noon*

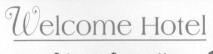

Welcome Hotel

Name *Claire Costello*

TIME CARD

Day		In
MONDAY	January 24	2:45 p.m.
TUESDAY	January 25	6:55 a.m.
WEDNESDAY	January 26	6:04 a.m.
THURSDAY	January 27	2:30 p.m.
FRIDAY	January 28	6:00 a.m.

1. Monday, January 24   *early*

2. Tuesday, January 25   _____

3. Wednesday, January 26   _____

4. Thursday, January 27   _____

5. Friday, January 28   _____

**B. Critical thinking. Claire Costello loves old
movies. She wants to see <u>King Kong</u>.
Look at the movie schedule.
Circle the times Claire can see <u>King Kong</u>.**

KING KONG

ARTS THEATER
MONDAY AND FRIDAY ONLY

Schedule of showings:
Monday 1/24: 6:00 p.m., 8:00 p.m., 10:30 p.m.
Friday 1/28: 4:45 p.m., 7:30 p.m., midnight

Monday, January 24.

A. Look at Dan Kim's date book for March 17. Answer the questions.

1. What time does work start? _____

2. When does English class start? _____

B. Complete the date book for yourself. Write about this week.

MONDAY

TUESDAY

WEDNESDAY

THURSDAY

FRIDAY

17
MARCH

8:00 to 4:00	
work	
12:00 to 1:00	
English class	
Meeting Room 1	

Dan Kim

➤ Do it yourself!   A plan-ahead project

Discussion. Bring a work schedule or a movie schedule to class. Or use the examples here and your date book from Exercise B. Talk about times and dates.

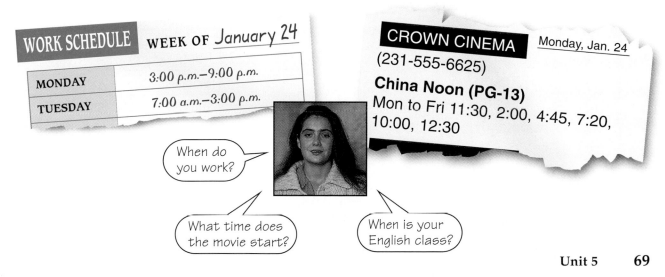

WORK SCHEDULE   WEEK OF *January 24*

| MONDAY | 3:00 p.m.–9:00 p.m. |
| TUESDAY | 7:00 a.m.–3:00 p.m. |

CROWN CINEMA   Monday, Jan. 24
(231-555-6625)
China Noon (PG-13)
Mon to Fri 11:30, 2:00, 4:45, 7:20, 10:00, 12:30

When do you work?

What time does the movie start?

When is your English class?

Review

A. **Vocabulary. Write the time with numbers.**

1. _____   2. _____   3. _____

B. **Conversation. Complete the conversations. Circle the letter.**

1. **A:** Bye.

   B: _____

   a. See you on Tuesday.   **b.** Oh, hi.

2. **A:** When does the movie start?

   B: _____

   a. On time.   **b.** At 4:30.

3. **A:** _____

   B: It's Thursday.

   a. What day is today?   **b.** What month is it?

C. **Grammar. Choose words. Write the words on the line.**

1. _____ 5:30?
   <u>Is / Is it</u>

2. _____ Monday.
   <u>Is / It's</u>

3. When _____ the English class?
   <u>it's / is</u>

4. What time _____?
   <u>it's / is it</u>

D. **Reading. Look at Paul Winston's date book and time card. On the time card circle the day he is late.**

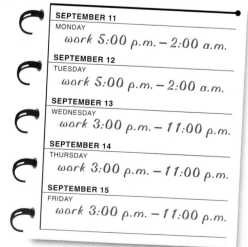

TIME CARD	
Paul Winston	**IN**
Monday	4:49 p.m.
Tuesday	5:00 p.m.
Wednesday	3:12 p.m.
Thursday	2:55 p.m.
Friday	3:00 p.m.

> **Do it yourself!**
>
> 1. Point. Talk about people and places.
>   *He's a bus driver.*
>   *The restaurant is next to the post office.*
>
> 2. Create conversations for the people.
>   *A: What time is it?*
>   *B: It's 8:35.*
>
> 3. Say more about the picture. Use your <u>own</u> words. Say as much as you can.

Now I can
❑ tell time.
❑ talk about days and dates.
❑ read and write schedules.
❑ _____.

Supplies and services

Vocabulary

Picture dictionary

🎧 A. Listen.

Foods and drinks

① an apple ⟷ ② apples	⑬ rice	⑭ lettuce
③ an onion ⟷ ④ onions	⑯ chicken	⑰ fish
⑤ a carrot ⟷ ⑥ carrots	⑲ bread	⑳ cheese
⑦ a bean ⟷ ⑧ beans	㉒ water	㉓ coffee
⑨ a tomato ⟷ ⑩ tomatoes	㉔ tea	㉕ sugar
⑪ an egg ⟷ ⑫ eggs		

⑮ meat
⑱ milk
㉑ juice

Actions

㉖ buy
㉗ eat

🎧 B. Listen again and repeat.

72   Unit 6

 **C.** Listen to the sentences. Look at the pictures.

a.   b.   c.

Now listen again. Write the letter of the picture on the line.

1. _____

2. _____

3. _____

D. Collaborative activity. Work with a partner. Write a shopping list for this food.

1. __bread__   2. _____

3. _____   4. __carrots__

5. _____   6. _____

7. _____   8. _____

> **Do it yourself!**

A. Ask your partner about foods. Complete the chart.

Paula, do you eat eggs?

FOOD	Paula		my partner	
	EATS	DOESN'T EAT	EATS	DOESN'T EAT
eggs	✓			
cheese		✓		
meat		✓		
fish	✓			

B. Tell the class about your partner. Then tell the class about yourself.

My partner eats cheese. I don't eat eggs.

Practical conversations

Model 1   Talk about supplies you need.

🎧 **A. Listen and read.**

> **A:** Hi, Tony. What's up?
> **B:** Not much. But we need two boxes of rice.
> **A:** Anything else?
> **B:** No, that's all.

🎧 **B. Listen again and repeat.**

C. Pair work. Now use the containers.

> **A:** Hi, _____. What's up?
> **B:** Not much. But we need a _____.
> **A:** Anything else?
> **B:** No, that's all.

🎧 **Containers**

a box of rice   **a bottle of** juice   **a bag of** onions   **a can of** coffee

Model 2   Talk about what you like. Agree and disagree.

🎧 **A. Listen and read.**

> **A:** I really like coffee.
> **B:** Not me. I like tea.
> **A:** And what about milk?
> **B:** I love milk.
> **A:** Me too!

🎧 **B. Listen again and repeat.**

C. Pair work. Now use words from the box and your <u>own</u> opinions.

juice	coffee	tea
lettuce	tomatoes	onions
meat	fish	chicken

A: I really like _____.

B: Not me. I like _____.

A: And what about _____?

B: I love _____.

A: Me too!

Model 3 Ask about supplies.

A. Listen and read.

A: Look in the supply room. Is there any juice?

B: Yes, there is.

A: And are there any onions?

B: No, there aren't. We're out of onions.

B. Listen again and repeat.

C. Pair work. Now use the pictures.

A: Look _____. Is there any _____?

B: Yes, there is.

A: And are there any _____?

B: No, there aren't. We're out of _____.

How to say it

in the refrigerator   on the shelf

Is there any _____?   Are there any _____?

➤ Do it yourself!

Pair work. Create a conversation from the pictures. Talk about the supplies on the shelves.

How many cans of coffee do we have?

Count and non-count nouns

Count nouns	Non-count nouns
a tomato tomatoes an apple apples	milk cheese
Count nouns use <u>a</u> and <u>an</u>. Count nouns have plural forms.	Non-count nouns do not use <u>a</u> and <u>an</u>. Non-count nouns do not have plural forms.

A. Write these words in the lists.

~~apple~~	~~rice~~	egg	meat
onion	carrot	cheese	tea

Count nouns

1. _apple_
2. _____
3. _____
4. _____

Non-count nouns

1. _rice_
2. _____
3. _____
4. _____

Questions with <u>How many</u> and <u>How much</u>

Use <u>How many</u> to ask questions about count nouns.
  How many eggs do you want?

Use <u>How much</u> to ask questions about non-count nouns.
  How much milk do you want?

B. Choose <u>How many</u> or <u>How much</u>. Write the words on the line.

1. _____ sugar do you want?
   How many / How much

2. _____ lettuce do you have?
   How many / How much

3. _____ onions do you have in the refrigerator?
   How many / How much

4. _____ cans of beans do we have on the shelf?
   How many / How much

5. _____ rice do we need?
   How many / How much

There is and There are

Use There is or There's with singular count nouns and all non-count nouns.
> **There's** an **apple** on the shelf. (singular count noun)
> **There's sugar** in this coffee. (non-count noun)

Use There are with plural nouns.
> **There are** four **onions** in that bag.

C. Choose There's or There are. Write the words on the line.

1. _____ six carrots in that bag.
   There's / There are

2. _____ a tomato in the refrigerator.
   There's / There are

3. _____ five boxes of apples on the shelf.
   There's / There are

4. _____ bread in the supply room.
   There's / There are

Questions with Are there any and Is there any

Are there any onions on the shelf?	Yes, there are. / No, there aren't.
Is there any milk in this tea?	Yes, there is. / No, there isn't.

D. Write questions with Are there any and Is there any.

1. sugar / in the supply room? *Is there any sugar in the supply room?*

2. beans / in the kitchen? _____

3. cheese / on the shelf? _____

4. tomatoes / in the restaurant? _____

➤ Do it yourself!

A. Pair work. Ask and answer questions about the picture. Use Is there any and Are there any.

A: *Are there any eggs in this picture?*
B: *Yes, there are.*

B. Personalization. Ask your partner questions about food and supplies. Use How much or How many.

How much juice do you have at home?

Authentic practice 1

With words you know, YOU can talk to this grocer.

🎧 **A. Listen and read.**

Grocer: Hi. How's it going?

YOU *OK, Mr. Rossi. What do you need today?*

Grocer: Well, let's start with a case of eggs.

YOU *OK. One case of eggs.*

Grocer: Actually, let's make that two cases of eggs, one large and one medium.

YOU *Two cases of eggs. What about tomatoes?*

Grocer: I'll take two boxes of those tomatoes from Mexico.

YOU *OK. Anything else?*

Grocer: No, I think that's all for today.

YOU *OK. Great, Mr. Rossi. Thanks.*

🎧 **B. Listen to the grocer. Read your part.**

🎧 **C. Listen and read. Choose your response. Circle the letter.**

1. "I need to buy a box of large tomatoes."

   a. One box of large tomatoes. OK.   **b.** I don't know.

2. "Let's start with coffee. Do you have any from Brazil?"

   a. Do you like milk in your coffee?   **b.** Yes, I think so.

3. "I think that's all for now."

   a. OK. See you later.   **b.** Anything else?

🎧 **D. Listen. Choose your response. Circle the letter.**

1. **a.** Yes, there is.   **b.** Do you want large or medium?

2. **a.** Not much.   **b.** How many boxes do you want?

3. **a.** OK. What do you want today?   **b.** How about rice?

A. Listen to the conversations. Then answer the questions. Circle the letter.

1. What's Jean's occupation?   **a.** cook   **b.** cashier

2. Where are the two people?   **a.** in a kitchen   **b.** at the office

B. Read the list of foods. Then listen to Conversation 1 again. Check ☑ the foods that are in the Super Salad.

☐ beans   ☐ lettuce   ☐ tomatoes   ☐ onions   ☐ chicken   ☐ cheese

C. Look at the pictures of the three sandwiches. Listen to Conversation 2 again.

a.   b.   c.

Now listen again. Circle the letter of the sandwich in the conversation.

➤ Do it yourself!

A. Write your <u>own</u> response. Then read your conversation out loud with a partner.

> We need bread. Please buy some when you're at the store.

YOU _____

> Do you think we need anything else?

YOU _____

> OK. See you later. Thanks.

YOU _____

B. Discussion. Talk about supplies you need or about foods you really like.

Reading

A. **Look at the box. What do you need to cook spaghetti?**

❑ water ❑ oil

❑ salt ❑ onions

❑ spaghetti ❑ sugar

B. **Critical thinking. Are the directions correct? Write yes or no.**

1	2	3
Put water in the pot.	Put 1 tablespoon of oil and 1 teaspoon of salt in the pot.	Boil the water.
4	5	6
Put the spaghetti in the boiling water.	Cook the spaghetti for 10 minutes.	Drain the spaghetti.

1. Put the spaghetti in the pot. Then boil the water. __no__

2. Cook the spaghetti. Then drain the spaghetti. _____

3. Put the water, salt, and oil in the pot. Then boil the water. _____

4. Drain the spaghetti. Then boil the water. _____

C. **Pair work. Tell your partner how to cook spaghetti.**

First, put water in a large pot.

A. Read the recipe for tomato bean soup.

Tomato Bean Soup

Ingredients

1 medium onion	2 cups of water
2 large carrots	2 15-ounce cans of tomatoes
1 tablespoon of oil	1 10-ounce can of small white beans

Directions

1. Chop the onion and carrots. Put the onion, carrots, and oil in a large pot. Cook for five minutes.
2. Put the water in the pot. Put the tomatoes in the pot. Cook for 30 minutes.
3. Put the beans in the pot. Cook for 10 minutes.

 Recipe words

chop

a cup

B. Critical thinking. Raquel Taylor wants to make tomato bean soup. What does she need? Look at the picture of the foods she has in her kitchen. Write a shopping list for her.

Shopping List

➤ Do it yourself!   A plan-ahead project

A. Discussion. Bring your own recipes to class. Talk about the recipes. Or use this recipe.

B. Collaborative activity. Work with a partner. Choose a recipe you like. Make a shopping list for that recipe.

Shopping List

apples

Fruit Salad

Ingredients

Apples	Oranges
Pears	Bananas

Directions

Cut the fruit in small pieces.
Put the fruit in a large bowl.
Serve and enjoy.

Review

A. **Vocabulary. Write a shopping list for the foods in the picture.**

shopping List

B. **Conversation. Choose _your_ response. Circle the letter.**

1. "Are we out of onions?"

   a. No, there's a bag on the shelf.   **b.** Not me.

2. "We need milk."

   a. How much do you want?   **b.** See you tomorrow.

3. "Do you need anything else?"

   a. Yes, I want bread, please.   **b.** Yes, me too.

C. **Grammar. Choose words. Write the words on the line.**

1. _____ coffee in this can.
   There's / There are

2. _____ two bags of rice in the supply room.
   There's / There are

3. _____ any juice in the refrigerator?
   Is there / Are there

4. _____ apples do we need?
   How much / How many

D. **Reading. Match the pictures with the directions. Write the letters on the lines.**

a.   **b.**   **c.**   **d.**

OLD TIME
• SOUP MIX •

TOMATO

DIRECTIONS:

1. _____ Put 2 cups of water in a pot.

2. _____ Boil the water.

3. _____ Put the soup mix in the water.

4. _____ Cook the soup for 10 minutes.

> **Do it yourself!**

1. Point. Name the foods and drinks.
   Onions

2. Point. Ask questions.
   How much juice does he have?

3. Create conversations for the people.
   A: Where's the coffee?
   B: In Aisle 2.

4. Say more about the picture. Use your <u>own</u> words. Say as much as you can.

AISLE 2

Now I can
☐ talk about foods.
☐ talk about likes and dislikes.
☐ follow recipes.
☐ _____.

Relationships

Objectives
- talk about what you're doing
- talk about what you can do
- talk about what you have to do
- tell people why

Vocabulary

Picture dictionary

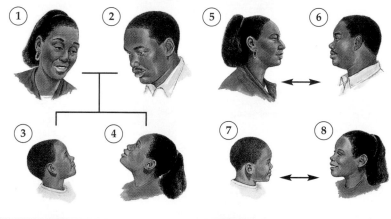

A. Listen.

Relationships		Actions	
① a mother	⑤ a wife	⑩ fix	⑮ stay home
② a father	⑥ a husband	⑪ install	⑯ study
③ a son	⑦ a brother	⑫ drive	⑰ come
④ a daughter	⑧ a sister	⑬ clean	⑱ go
	⑨ friends	⑭ work	

B. Listen again and repeat.

84   Unit 7

🎧 **C.** **Look at the pictures. Listen to the sentences. Then listen again.**
Match the pictures and the sentences. Write the letter on the line.

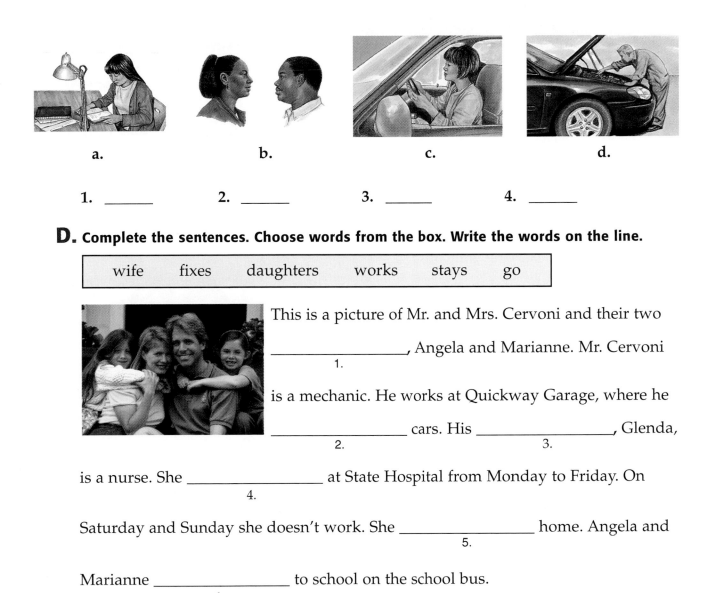

a.   b.   c.   d.

1. _____   2. _____   3. _____   4. _____

D. **Complete the sentences. Choose words from the box. Write the words on the line.**

wife	fixes	daughters	works	stays	go

This is a picture of Mr. and Mrs. Cervoni and their two
_____, Angela and Marianne. Mr. Cervoni
     1.

is a mechanic. He works at Quickway Garage, where he
_____ cars. His _____, Glenda,
     2.   3.

is a nurse. She _____ at State Hospital from Monday to Friday. On
               4.

Saturday and Sunday she doesn't work. She _____ home. Angela and
                                                     5.

Marianne _____ to school on the school bus.
              6.

> ➤ Do it yourself!

A. **Complete the chart. Write about two friends or two people in your family.**

Name	Relationship	Occupation	Workplace
Dan	brother	cook	restaurant
1.			
2.			

B. **Tell the class about your friends or family.**
Dan is my brother. He's a cook. He works in a restaurant.

Practical conversations

🎧 **A.** Listen and read.

> **A:** Are you busy right now?
> **B:** Yes, I am.
> **A:** What are you doing?
> **B:** I'm working.

🎧 **B.** Listen again and repeat.

C. Pair work. **Now use the pictures.**

> **A:** Are you busy right now?
> **B:** Yes, I am.
> **A:** What are you doing?
> **B:** I'm _____.

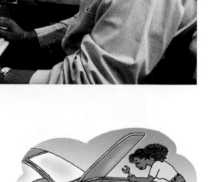

cleaning   studying   fixing the car

Model 2   Explain what you have to do.

🎧 **A.** Listen and read.

> **A:** Are you ready to go?
> **B:** No, I'm sorry. Not yet.
> **A:** Why not?
> **B:** Because I have to fix the computer.
> **A:** OK.

🎧 **B.** Listen again and repeat.

C. Pair work. **Now use your <u>own</u> words.**

> **A:** Are you ready to go?
> **B:** No, I'm sorry. Not yet.
> **A:** Why not?
> **B:** Because I have to _____.
> **A:** _____.

🎧 **A.** **Listen and read.**

A: Can John clean the meeting room?
B: No, I'm sorry. He can't.
A: Why?
B: Because he's at the post office right now.
A: Well, when can he clean the meeting room?
B: In an hour.

🎧 **B.** **Listen again and repeat.**

C. Pair work. **Now use actions from the box and your own words.**

| install the telephones | clean the kitchen | fix the computer |

A: Can _____?
B: No, I'm sorry. _____ can't.
A: Why?
B: Because _____.
A: Well, when can _____?
B: In _____.

🎧 **How to say it**

in an hour   in 10 minutes

➤ **Do it yourself!**

Pair work. **Continue the conversation for the people in the picture.**

Are you ready to eat?

The present continuous

Use the present continuous to talk about right now.

A: What **are** you **doing** right now?

B: I'm busy. I**'m working**.

I'm	
You're	
He's	**working.**
She's	

We're	
You're	**working.**
They're	

Questions

Is he **fixing** the bus?

Are you **studying** English?

Answers

Yes, he is. /
No, he's not.

Yes, I am. /
No, I'm not.

A. **Choose a word. Write the word on the line.**

1. _____ Pedro fixing the lawn mower?
   <u>Is / Are</u>

2. Is Lana _____ that book?
   <u>read / reading</u>

3. What _____ they doing now?
   <u>is / are</u>

4. Who's _____ room 22?
   <u>clean / cleaning</u>

5. Are you _____ the shelves in the kitchen or the supply room?
   <u>install / installing</u>

B. **Complete each sentence with the present continuous. Write the words on the line.**

1. I'm busy. I _____.
   <u>work</u>

2. Rafael can't clean the meeting room. He _____ the telephones.
   <u>fix</u>

3. We're not ready. We _____ the kitchen.
   <u>clean</u>

Can and can't

He **can fix** copiers.   He **can't fix** cars.

Don't use <u>to</u> with <u>can</u>: I can drive.

Questions

Can you go tomorrow?

What can you do?

Who can help my friend?

Answers

Yes, I can. / No, I can't.

I can write recipes.

Al can.

C. **Ask your partner these questions. Then write about your partner.**

1. Can you drive?

2. What can you fix?

1. My partner _____.

2. My partner _____.

Have to and don't have to

She **has to work** on Monday.

MONDAY

She **doesn't have to work** on Sunday.

SUNDAY

Do you have to return that uniform?   Yes, I do. / No, I don't.
Why does Juan have to work on Sunday?   Because he can't work on Monday.

D. **Choose** **have to** **or** **has to**. **Write the words on the line.**

1. I _____ start the coffee maker in 10 minutes. Do you have that can of coffee?

have to / has to

2. Who _____ clean the shelves in the supply room? Is it you or Gonzalo?

have to / has to

3. Why do you _____ call the store? Is that paper the wrong color?

have to / has to

4. The electricians don't _____ install the copiers today. Tomorrow's OK.

have to / has to

➤Do it yourself!

A. **Personalization.**
Complete your date book for next week.

MONDAY
go to the supermarket

B. **Pair work.**
Ask and answer questions about your schedule.

Can you go to the movies on Friday?

No, I can't. I have to work on Friday.

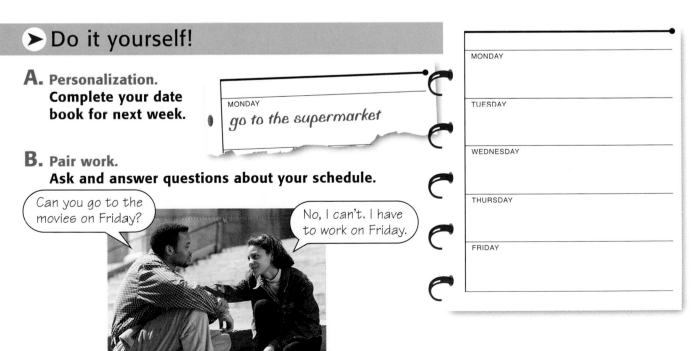

MONDAY
TUESDAY
WEDNESDAY
THURSDAY
FRIDAY

Authentic practice 1

With words you know, YOU can talk to this manager.

🎧 **A.** Listen and read.

Manager: I know you don't work on Saturdays, but do you think you could work tomorrow? Tom's taking a personal day because his son is in the hospital.

YOU *Oh, I'm sorry. . . . No problem. I can work tomorrow. What do you need?*

Manager: Someone has to install the new telephones in the King Street building. You can do that, can't you?

YOU *Sure. I can install telephones.*

Manager: That's great! See you tomorrow, then. And thanks a million.

YOU *You're welcome.*

🎧 **B.** Listen to the manager. Read <u>your</u> part.

🎧 **C.** Listen and read. Choose <u>your</u> response. Circle the letter.

1. "What do you have to do?"

   a. Because I'm busy.   **b.** I have to fix the copier.

2. "Are you busy?"

   a. No. What do you need?   **b.** Thanks.

3. "You can do that later, can't you?"

   a. Yes, I can.   **b.** Not yet.

🎧 **D.** Listen. Choose <u>your</u> response. Circle the letter.

1. **a.** Is he OK?   **b.** I'm too busy right now.

2. **a.** Not yet.   **b.** No, I'm sorry. I can't.

3. **a.** OK.   **b.** Not me.

A. Listen to the conversation. Then complete the sentences. Circle the letter.

1. The two people are _____.

   a. a husband and a wife   **b.** an employee and a manager

2. They're talking about _____.

   a. a personal day   **b.** supplies

B. Read the sentences. Then listen again. Complete each sentence with <u>Claire</u> or <u>Boris</u>.

1. _____ has to take a personal day.

2. _____ has to buy a car.

3. _____ has to install the exit doors.

4. _____ can clean the meeting rooms at 6:00.

C. Discussion. Listen again. Talk about Boris's problem. Use the pictures and your <u>own</u> words.

➤ Do it yourself!

A. Write your <u>own</u> response. Then read your conversation out loud with a partner.

 Are you very busy right now?

YOU _____

 I need some help.

YOU _____

 I need someone to take these supplies to the office. Can you do that?

YOU _____

B. Discussion. Talk about what you have to do at work or at home.

Reading

A. Read the personal day policy from the Quality Paint Company.

Quality Paint Company

Personal Day Policy

Every employee is entitled to 4 paid personal days a year.
When you can't come to work, you MUST:

- Call or speak to your manager one day BEFORE the personal day.
  For example: If you need to take a personal day on Wednesday, you have to tell your manager on Tuesday.
- Tell your manager the date you can return to work.
- Fill out a personal day form when you return to work.

B. **Critical thinking.** **Read about these employees of the Quality Paint Company. Are they following the company policy for personal days? Write <u>yes</u> or <u>no</u>.**

Hakeem

1. Michael Hakeem has to buy a new car. On Monday morning, he tells his manager he can't come to work on Tuesday, March 13. On Wednesday, when he returns, he fills out a personal day form. _____

Johnson

2. On Wednesday, March 14, Lucy Johnson can't go to work. She doesn't tell her manager. She stays home. When she returns on Thursday, she fills out the personal day form. _____

Lara

3. Today is Friday, March 15. Andrea Lara tells her manager she can't come to work next week. When Andrea returns, she fills out a personal day form for five days. _____

A. Read Renee Samadi's personal day form. Then read the sentences. Write <u>yes</u> or <u>no</u>.

Quality Paint Company

Personal Day Form

Employee: _Renee Samadi_   Department: _Quality Control_

Date(s) of absence: _May 22_   Date of return to work: _May 23_

Reason: _My husband is very sick. I have to take my husband to the doctor._

1. Renee Samadi's personal day is May 23. _____

2. Renee Samadi works in the Quality Control Department. _____

3. Renee Samadi's husband needs to go to the doctor. _____

B. Read about Michael Hakeem again in Exercise B on page 92. Mr. Hakeem works in the Sales Department. Fill out his personal day form.

Quality Paint Company

Personal Day Form

Employee: _____   Department: _____

Date(s) of absence: _____   Date of return to work: _____

Reason: _____

➤ Do it yourself!

Take a personal day. Complete the personal day form for yourself.

Quality Paint Company

Personal Day Form

Employee: _____   Department: _Customer Service_

Date(s) of absence: _____   Date of return to work: _____

Reason: _____

 **Review**

A. Vocabulary. Choose words to complete the sentences. Write the words on the line.

Marie and Paul Martin have a _____, Peter, and a daughter, Nicole. Paul
_____
1. husband / son

is the father, and Marie is the _____. Marie _____ at the North
_____   _____
2. mother / daughter   3. installs / works

Side Hospital. She is a nurse. Tomorrow Marie is _____, and she can't go to
_____
4. busy / ready

work. She _____ take a personal day.
_____
5. has / has to

B. Conversation. Choose your response. Circle the letter.

1. "When can you go to the supply room?"

   a. In 15 minutes.   **b.** Because I'm too busy.

2. "Why are you late today?"

   a. In an hour.   **b.** Because my husband is in the hospital.

3. "What are you doing now?"

   a. I'm working.   **b.** I'm ready.

C. Grammar. Choose words. Write the words on the line.

1. Who _____ this bus? Walter?
        driving / is driving

2. I can't clean the office now. I _____ go to the bank.
                                    have to / don't have to

3. Can you _____ to the supermarket? We're out of milk.
            to go / go

D. Reading. Read the personal day form. Then write yes, no, or I don't know.

Galaxy Garden Supplies .... **Personal Day Form**

Employee: _____*Valerie Lavin*_____

Today's date: _____*August 3*_____   Date(s) of absence: _____*August 4*_____

Reason: ___*My son has to go to the doctor.*___

1. The employee is Valerie Lavin's son. _____

2. The personal day is August 4. _____

3. Valerie has a daughter. _____

➤ **Do it yourself!**

1. Point. Name the relationships.
   Father, daughter

2. Point. What are the people doing?
   She's studying.

3. Create conversations for the people.
   A: *What are you doing?*
   B: *I'm fixing the door.*

4. Say more about the picture. Use your <u>own</u> words. Say as much as you can.

Now I can
❑ talk about what I'm doing.
❑ talk about what I can do.
❑ talk about what I have to do.
❑ tell people why.
❑ _____.

Health and safety

Vocabulary

Picture dictionary

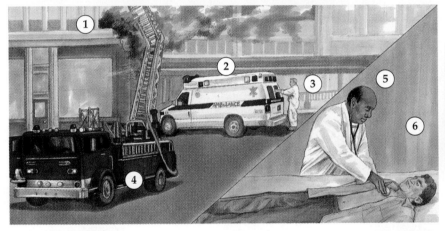

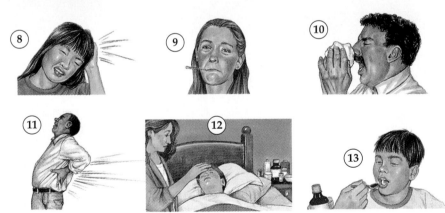

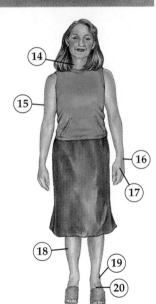

🎧 **A.** Listen.

Health and safety			**Parts of the body**	
① a fire	⑥ an emergency room	⑩ have a cold	⑭ a neck	⑱ a leg
② an ambulance	⑦ an accident	⑪ have a backache	⑮ an arm	⑲ an ankle
③ a paramedic	⑧ have a headache	⑫ have the flu	⑯ a wrist	⑳ a foot
④ a fire truck	⑨ have a fever	⑬ take medicine	⑰ a hand	
⑤ a doctor				

🎧 **B.** Listen again and repeat.

C. Listen to the conversations. What's the problem? Circle the letter.

1. a.   b.

2. a.  b.

3. a.  b.

D. Choose words. Write the words on the line.

1. Linda hurt her _____, and now she can't write.
   <u>foot / hand</u>

2. Ms. Yin hurt her back. She has to go to _____.
   <u>the doctor / the accident</u>

3. Mr. Ortiz has the flu. He has to take _____.
   <u>medicine / an ambulance</u>

4. There's _____ on Park Avenue. Call a fire truck!
   <u>a fire / a doctor</u>

➤ Do it yourself!

A. Read the health problems. Then complete the chart.

> When I have a cold, I eat chicken soup and I drink tea.

Problem	Medicine	Foods	Drinks
a cold	I take aspirin.	I eat chicken soup.	I drink tea.
a backache			
the flu			
a headache			

B. Discussion. Talk about the health problems and what you do.

Model 1 Make a phone call.

🎧 **A. Listen and read.**

A: Hello?

B: Hi, Dan. This is Bill. Can you talk?

A: Well, I'm fixing a door right now. I'm sorry. Can I call you back?

B: Sure. No problem. Talk to you later.

A: Thanks. Bye.

B: Bye.

🎧 **B. Listen again and repeat.**

C. Pair work. Now use your <u>own</u> words.

A: Hello?

B: Hi, _____. This is _____. Can you talk?

A: Well, I'm _____ right now. I'm sorry. Can I call you back?

B: Sure. No problem. Talk to you later.

A: Thanks. Bye.

B: Bye.

Model 2 Make an appointment.

🎧 **A. Listen and read.**

A: Doctor Baker's office. How can I help you?

B: This is Dan Kim. I need to make an appointment. I hurt my back.

A: Oh, I'm sorry. How about tomorrow at 9:30?

B: Tomorrow at 9:30? That's fine. See you then.

A: Feel better!

B: Thanks a lot.

🎧 **B. Listen again and repeat.**

C. Pair work. Now use your <u>own</u> words.

A: Doctor _____ 's office. How can I help you?

B: I need to make an appointment. I _____.

A: Oh, I'm sorry. How about _____ at _____?

B: _____? That's finc. See you then.

A: Feel better!

B: _____.

🎧 **Health problems**

I hurt my back.
I hurt my foot.
I have the flu.
I have a backache.

Model 3   Make a 911 call.

🎧 **A. Listen and read.**

A: This is 911.

B: There's an accident at the corner of
Front Street and Third Avenue.

A: Do you need an ambulance or a fire truck?

B: An ambulance, please.

A: OK. It's on its way.

🎧 **B. Listen again and repeat.**

C. Pair work. Now use your <u>own</u> words.

A: This is 911.

B: There's _____ at _____.

A: Do you need _____?

B: _____.

➤ Do it yourself!

Pair work. **Create a conversation from the pictures. Use your <u>own</u> words.**

Practical grammar

Possessives

A. **Choose words. Write the words on the line.**

1. This is my daughter, and _____ name is Sonia.
   his / her

2. I have to call Shardul and Clara. Do you have _____ phone number?
   his / their

3. He has two offices. _____ new office is on Smith Street.
   His / Their

4. This is _____ old uniform. It's too small.
   Fran / Fran's

Never, sometimes, always

0% **never**	**sometimes**	100% **always**

Use the simple present tense with <u>never</u>, <u>sometimes</u>, and <u>always</u>.
   I **sometimes drink** coffee.
<u>Never</u>, <u>sometimes</u>, and <u>always</u> go before the simple present tense verb.
   I **never drink** tea.
<u>Never</u>, <u>sometimes</u>, and <u>always</u> go after forms of the verb <u>be</u>.
   I'm **never** busy.

B. **Answer the questions. Use <u>never</u>, <u>sometimes</u>, or <u>always</u>.**

1. What do you take when you have a headache? *I always take aspirin.*

2. Do you drink tea? _____

3. Are you busy on Saturdays? _____

4. Do you go to the emergency room when you have the flu? _____

The simple present tense and the present continuous

Use the simple present tense with <u>have</u>, <u>want</u>, <u>need</u>, and <u>like</u>.
   I **like** that store.
Use the simple present tense with <u>never</u>, <u>sometimes</u>, and <u>always</u>.
   I always **eat** early.

Don't use the present continuous with <u>never</u>, <u>sometimes</u>, and <u>always</u>.
Use the present continuous to talk about what you are doing right now.
   What are you doing? I'**m talking** to the doctor.

C. **Choose the present continuous or the simple present tense. Write the words on the line.**

1. Mario _____ a backache.
              has / is having

2. He always _____ that bus.
                  drives / is driving

3. Do you _____ an ambulance?
             need / needing

4. I'm _____ the doctor right now.
           call / calling

D. **Complete the chart about yourself and a friend or a family member. Then tell the class about one person.**

Name	Has colds	Has headaches	Takes medicine
Tasha	never	sometimes	sometimes
1.			
2.			

➤ Do it yourself!

Point. Talk about the picture.
He hurt his arm. He hurt his head.

Authentic practice 1

With words you know, YOU can talk to this nurse.

🎧 **A.** Listen and read.

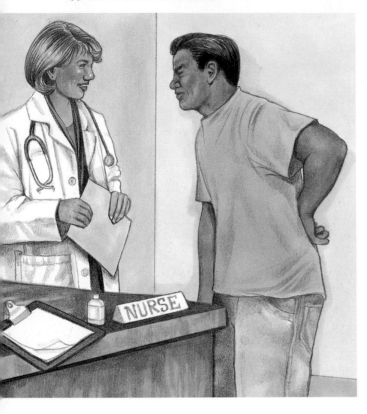

Nurse: How can I help you?

YOU *I hurt my back at work.*

Nurse: Oh, I'm sorry. Does it hurt anywhere else? What about down your leg?

YOU *Down my leg? Yes. Down my right leg.*

Nurse: Well, a doctor can see you in about an hour. First, let me give you some medicine. Can you take aspirin?

YOU *Yes. I always take aspirin.*

Nurse: OK, take these two aspirins. Have a seat, and please fill out this form. And I hope you feel better soon.

YOU *Thanks a lot.*

🎧 **B.** Listen to the nurse. Read <u>your</u> part.

🎧 **C.** Listen and read. Choose <u>your</u> response. Circle the letter.

1. "How can I help you?"
   a. Not me.   **b.** I need to see the doctor.

2. "What's the problem?"
   a. I hurt my right arm.   **b.** That's OK.

3. "Feel better soon."
   a. Thank you.   **b.** You're welcome.

🎧 **D.** Listen. Choose <u>your</u> response. Circle the letter.

1. **a.** Yes, sure. It hurts here.   **b.** Dr. Smith's office.

2. **a.** Yes, I can. Thank you.   **b.** Can I call you back?

3. **a.** Me too.   **b.** OK, thanks.

A. Listen to the conversation. Then complete the sentences. Circle the letter.

1. The women are _____.

   a. on the telephone   **b.** in a van

2. They are _____.

   a. doctors   **b.** friends

B. Read the questions. Then listen again. Listen for numbers in the conversation. Circle the letter.

1. What time was the accident?

   a. 8:30   **b.** 9:00

2. How many people were in the van?

   a. 1   **b.** 3

3. How many people in the van were hurt?

   a. 2   **b.** 3

4. How many paramedics were in the ambulance?

   a. 1   **b.** 2

➤ Do it yourself!

A. Write your <u>own</u> response. Then read your conversation out loud with a partner.

Hello?

YOU _____

You sound terrible. What's the problem?

YOU _____

Oh, I'm so sorry. I hope you feel better soon.

YOU _____

B. Discussion. Talk about your health or the health of a family member.

Reading

A. Read Mr. Reyes's accident report. Then check ☑ the boxes. What information does the report ask for?

1. ☐ the worker's name
2. ☐ the worker's address
3. ☐ the worker's date of birth
4. ☐ the worker's place of birth
5. ☐ the worker's phone number
6. ☐ the doctor's name

B. Critical thinking. Look at the two ways to write dates. Then answer the questions. Circle the letter.

Words and numbers	Numbers
August 2, 1955	8/2/55
January 12, 2000	1/12/00

Totally Cool Air Conditioners

—— **Accident Report** ——

Employee: _____ Reyes _____ Carlos _____
             (last name)   (first name)

Date of birth: ___11___ ___3___ ___67___
            month   day   year

Complete the following section:

Date of accident: ___5___ ___13___ ___01___
            month   day   year

Place of accident (check one) ☑ at job ☐ other

Injury is to (check one)
☑ back or neck   ☐ ankle or foot
☐ hand or wrist   ☐ head
☐ leg   ☐ other

1. Why do we write August 2, 1955 as 8/2/55?

   a. Because August is the eighth month of the year.

   b. Because August is the second month of the year.

2. What is the year in 1/12/00?

   a. 2000.

   b. 2001.

C. Write the following dates with numbers.

1. November 3, 1983 _____
2. August 3, 2002 _____
3. June 24, 1986 _____
4. May 13, 2006 _____

D. Personalization. Complete the form about yourself. Write the dates in numbers.

Date of birth: _____

Today's date: _____

Read about Mary Costa's accident. Then complete the emergency room report form.

On Monday, June 14, 2001, Mary Costa had an accident on her way to work. The accident was at the corner of King Street and North Avenue. She hurt her neck.

Important information

- Ms. Costa's address is 84 North Avenue, Madison, New York.

- Her zip code is 10514.

- Her date of birth is September 8, 1944.

- Her phone number is (913) 555-6744.

✳ Memorial Hospital

Emergency Room	Patient Information

Patient's name: _____
             first   last or family

Date of visit: _____
           month   day   year

Address: _____
           number and street   city   state   zip code

Date of birth: _____
         month   day   year

Telephone: _____
           area code   number

➤ Do it yourself!

Pair work. Create a conversation between the receptionist and the patient. Use the picture for ideas. Use your <u>own</u> words.

Review

A. Vocabulary. Write the name of each body part on the line.

1. _____   2. _____   3. _____

4. _____   5. _____   6. _____

B. Conversation. Choose <u>your</u> response. Circle the letter.

1. "Can you talk?"

   a. Not now. I'm sorry.   **b.** This is Ray.

2. "Can I call you back later?"

   a. Not now. I'm eating.   **b.** Sure. How about 1:00?

3. "How's Wednesday?"

   a. She's fine.   **b.** Fine. See you then.

C. Grammar. Choose words. Write the words on the line.

1. "Doctor _____ office. How may I help you?"
   Stern / Stern's

2. Ms. Loyola hurt _____ foot in the accident.
   her / their

3. He _____ on the phone right now.
   talks / is talking

4. Juan sometimes _____ to work early.
   is going / goes

D. Reading. Read the report. Then write <u>yes</u>, <u>no</u>, or <u>I don't know</u>.

1. This is a report of a telephone call.

   _____

2. The car is Sharon Wong's car.

   _____

3. The date of the call is November 3, 2001.

   _____

4. Two people are hurt.

   _____

CENTER CITY
911 Report

Date: _10/3/01_

Time: _2:56 p.m._

Caller's name: _Sharon Wong_

Place: _corner of Park Street and Main Street_

Problem: _car fire_

> ➤ **Do it yourself!**

1. Point. Name things in the picture.
   An ambulance

2. Point. Talk about the people.
   She hurt her back.

3. Create conversations for the people.
   A: There's an accident on Grand Avenue.
   B: Do you need a fire truck?

4. Say more about the picture. Use your <u>own</u> words. Say as much as you can.

Now I can
❏ talk about accidents.
❏ talk about health.
❏ call 911.
❏ make an appointment.
❏ _____.

Money

Vocabulary

Picture dictionary

🎧 **A.** Listen.

Money and payment		Actions	Other words
① cash	⑤ an ATM	⑨ pay	⑭ cheap
② a check	⑥ an ATM card	⑩ pay by mail	⑮ expensive
③ a money order	⑦ a paycheck	⑪ cash a check	
④ a credit card	⑧ a bill	⑫ charge	
		⑬ go shopping	

🎧 **B.** Listen again and repeat.

C. Listen to the conversations. Look at the pictures. Then listen again and match. Write the letter of the picture on the line.

a.　　　　　　　b.　　　　　　　c.　　　　　　　d.

1. _____　　　2. _____　　　3. _____　　　4. _____

D. Complete the sentences. Write the words on the line.

1. Let's _____ our paychecks at the bank. Then we can go shopping.

2. I need to go to the post office to buy a _____. I want to send some money to my father in Mexico.

3. I like to talk on the telephone, but I don't like to pay the _____!

4. The store wants $50 for that book? That's too _____.

➤ Do it yourself!

A. Complete the chart.

Coins		Bills	
a penny	$ .01		$ 1.00
a nickel	$_____		$_____
a dime	$_____		$_____
a quarter	$_____		$_____

B. Collaborative activity. Complete the chart.

Amount	Possible combinations
$1.00	4 quarters, 10 dimes, 5 dimes and 2 quarters, 100 pennies
$2.50	
$34.99	

C. Discussion. Discuss your combinations with the class.

Practical conversations

Model 1 Ask for change.

A. Listen and read.

> **A:** Do you have change for five dollars?
> **B:** Let me check. Yes, I do. Here you go.
> **A:** Thanks.

B. Listen again and repeat.

C. Pair work. **Now answer <u>Yes, I do</u> or <u>No, I'm sorry. I don't</u>. Use the pictures.**

> **A:** Do you have change for _____?
> **B:** Let me check. _____.
> **A:** _____.

Model 2 Ask for a price.

A. Listen and read.

> **A:** Excuse me. How much is this lawn mower?
> **B:** $300.
> **A:** That's a lot. I'll have to think about it.

> **Problems with prices**
>
> a lot
> too expensive
> not cheap

B. Listen again and repeat.

C. Pair work. **Now use the pictures or your <u>own</u> words.**

> **A:** Excuse me. How much is this _____?
> **B:** _____.
> **A:** That's _____. I'll have to think about it.

A. **Listen and read.**

> **A:** How much is this TV?
> **B:** Only $85.99. It's on sale.
> **A:** Great. I'll take it.
> **B:** Will that be cash or charge?
> **A:** Cash.

B. **Listen again and repeat.**

C. Pair work. **Now use the pictures and your <u>own</u> prices.**

How to say it

- "Eighty-five ninety-nine"
 or
- "Eighty-five dollars and ninety-nine cents"

> **A:** How much is this _____?
> **B:** Only _____. It's on sale.
> **A:** Great. I'll take it.
> **B:** Will that be cash or charge?
> **A:** _____.

➤ Do it yourself!

Pair work. **Create a conversation from the picture. Use your <u>own</u> prices.**

The future

Tomorrow	I'm you're he's she's we're they're	going to buy a car.

What **are you going to do** tomorrow?
Who**'s going to cash** this check today?

A. Complete the sentences with a form of <u>be going to</u> and the verb.

1. I*'m going to charge* these clothes with my Quick Buy credit card.
   _{charge}

2. I_____ my paycheck, and then I'm going to go shopping.
   _{cash}

3. Next month we_____ new telephones.
   _{install}

4. Who_____ all these bills?
   _{pay}

5. Why_____ you _____ a car?
   _{buy}

B. Pair work. Ask your partner questions about the future. Use <u>be going to</u>.

1. What are you going to do today?
2. What are you going to do next year?

Now tell the class about your partner.

Next year Miriam is going to go to Mexico.

<u>Whose</u> and review of question words

Whose
Whose check is this?   It's Carla's check.
Whose shoes are these?   They're my shoes.

C. Complete the conversations with question words.

1. **A:** _____ car is in the parking lot?

   B: Bill's.

2. **A:** _____ are you going to do at the bank?

   B: I'm going to ask for change for a twenty-dollar bill.

3. **A:** _____ are you going to be ready?

   B: I don't know. I'm really busy right now.

4. **A:** _____ can't you charge this jacket?

   B: Because I don't have a credit card.

D. Form teams. Write questions for each answer in the box. Each question receives 1 point. You have five minutes.

Answers		
~~Fourteen.~~	She's my daughter.	Next year.
Brazil.	$2.50, I think.	A large salad.
Because they're on sale.	I don't know.	The supply room.

A: How many bills do you have to pay?
B: Fourteen.

➤ Do it yourself!

A. Pair work. Point. Ask questions about the future.

Is she going to return the jacket?

B. Personalization. Talk to your partner about shopping.

I'm going to buy shoes tomorrow.

With words you know, YOU can talk to this cashier.

🎧 **A.** Listen and read.

Cashier: That'll be $23.68, including the tax. Will that be cash or charge?

YOU *What about a check?*

Cashier: Sure. Is it from a local bank?

YOU *Excuse me?*

Cashier: Where is the check from? What bank?

YOU *Oh. It's from the First State Bank. On Clinton Avenue.*

Cashier: That's fine. I'll need to see some kind of I.D.

YOU *Is a driver's license OK?*

Cashier: Yes, that's great. Go ahead and write the check.

YOU *Here you go.*

Cashier: Thank you. And have a nice day.

🎧 **B.** Listen to the cashier. Read <u>your</u> part.

🎧 **C.** Listen and read. Choose <u>your</u> response. Circle the letter.

🎧 **I.D.**

a driver's license

a check-cashing card

1. "Cash or charge?"

   a. Is a check OK?   **b.** Yes.

2. "Do you have I.D.?"

   a. I'll take it.   **b.** Let me check. . . . Yes, here you go.

3. "That'll be $200."

   a. No problem.   **b.** Do you have change?

🎧 **D.** Listen. Choose <u>your</u> response. Circle the letter.

1. **a.** It's next to the parking lot.   **b.** Yes, it is.

2. **a.** Sure. Here you go.   **b.** Where are you going?

3. **a.** Thanks. Bye.   **b.** It's on sale.

🎧 **A.** **Listen to the conversation. Then read the sentences. Write _yes_ or _no_.**

1. The two people talking are a father and a daughter. _____

2. The man pays cash. _____

🎧 **B.** **Read the questions and answers. Then listen again to answer each question. Circle the letter.**

1. Who is paying the bill?

   a. Janet Klein.   **b.** Janet Klein's father.

2. Where are the people who are talking?

   a. In an office in Korea.   **b.** In an office in the United States.

3. Whose bill is it?

   a. Janet Klein's.   **b.** Mr. Klein's.

4. How much is the bill?

   a. $50.   **b.** $45.88.

5. Why does the man want quarters?

   a. He's going to pay the bill.   **b.** He's going to need quarters in the parking lot.

➤ Do it yourself!

A. **Write your _own_ response. Then read your conversation out loud with a partner.**

Is that check from a local bank?

YOU _____

Now I'll have to see some form of I.D.

YOU _____

Great. Thank you very much. Have a nice day.

YOU _____

B. **Discussion. Talk about your I.D. or about bills you have to pay.**

Reading

A. Look at the bill for newspaper delivery. Then check ☑ the information you can find on the bill.

1. ☐ the name of the newspaper
2. ☐ the amount the customer has to pay
3. ☐ the customer's telephone number
4. ☐ the newspaper's address
5. ☐ the customer's address
6. ☐ the date payment is due

B. Look at Larry Wilson's check. Circle and number these things:

1. the delivery dates
2. the amount of money in numbers
3. the amount of money in words
4. the date of the check

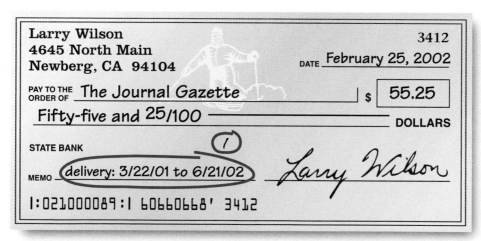

C. Critical thinking. Check ☑ the answer.

Mr. Wilson's payment is _____.

☐ early ☐ on time ☐ late

Look at the bill and receipt. Then complete the checks.

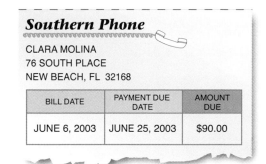

Southern Phone

CLARA MOLINA
76 SOUTH PLACE
NEW BEACH, FL 32168

BILL DATE	PAYMENT DUE DATE	AMOUNT DUE
JUNE 6, 2003	JUNE 25, 2003	$90.00

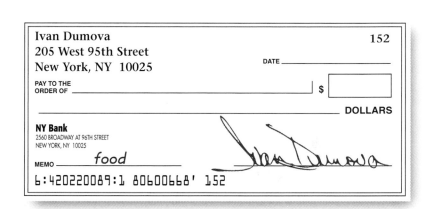

Clara Molina   257
76 South Place
New Beach, FL 32168   DATE _____

PAY TO THE
ORDER OF _____ $ _____

_____ DOLLARS

MEMO _____ *phone bill* _____   *Clara Molina*

7:02103009:1 800668' 257   **STATE BANK ⬥**

The Food Basket

August 16, 2003

Cheese	4.59
Eggs	1.89
Onions	0.99
Chicken soup	0.79
Meat	7.54
Subtotal	15.80
Tax	0.00
Amount due	$15.80

Ivan Dumova   152
205 West 95th Street
New York, NY 10025   DATE _____

PAY TO THE
ORDER OF _____ $ _____

_____ DOLLARS

NY Bank
2560 BROADWAY AT 96TH STREET
NEW YORK, NY 10025

MEMO _____ *food* _____

6:420220089:1 80600668' 152

➤ Do it yourself!   A plan-ahead project

Discussion. Bring a bill to class. Compare your bills. Use the pictures for ideas.

The Journal Gazette
P.O. Box 2274, Elk City, CA 94129-2267

CUSTOMER SERVICE NUMBER
1-800-555-1010

ACCOUNT NUMBER
WT42654

LARRY WILSON
4645 NORTH MAIN
NEWBERG, CA 94104

DELIVERY PERIOD
3/22/02

The Food Basket
August 16, 2003

Cheese	4.59
Eggs	1.89
Onions	0.99
Chicken soup	0.79
Meat	7.54
Subtotal	15.80
Tax	0.00
Amount due	$15.80

Ivan Dumova
205 West 95th Street
New York, NY 10025   DATE _____

PAY TO THE
ORDER OF _____ $ _____

_____ DOLLARS

NY Bank
2560 BROADWAY AT 96TH STREET
NEW YORK, NY 10025

MEMO _____ *food* _____

6:420220089:1 80600668' 152

What kind of bill is it?

Can you pay the bill with a check?

How are you going to pay the bill?

Quick Pay
1234 5687 3214 0000
10/99-08/02 M
TERRY M. DENZOLIS
Quick Pay

Review

A. **Vocabulary. Choose words. Write the words on the line.**

1. Is that cash, check, or _____?
   <u>charge / mail</u>

2. He's going to _____ his paycheck at the bank.
   <u>charge / cash</u>

3. I'm going to get some money from the _____.
   <u>ATM / bill</u>

4. I have a lot of _____ to pay this month.
   <u>cash / bills</u>

B. **Conversation. Choose <u>your</u> response. Circle the letter.**

1. "Do you have change for a dollar?"

   a. I'll have to think about it.   **b.** Yes, I do. Are four quarters OK?

2. "Will that be cash or charge?"

   a. It's my paycheck.   **b.** Is a check OK?

3. "I'll take it."

   a. Good. Will that be cash or charge?   **b.** I'll have to check.

C. **Grammar. Complete each sentence with a form of <u>be going to</u> and the verb.**

1. Tomorrow I`*m going to go shopping* for new shoes.
   <u>go shopping</u>

2. They _____ a check to the telephone company.
   <u>write</u>

3. When _____ you _____ your paycheck?
   <u>cash</u>

4. How much _____ they _____ for that car?
   <u>pay</u>

D. **Writing. Write a check to pay this bill.**

Food City	
Bread	1.00
Paper towels	3.00
Chicken	9.31
Subtotal	$13.31
Tax	$0.34
Amount due	$13.65

304

DATE _____

PAY TO THE
ORDER OF _____ | $ [   ]

_____ DOLLARS

Main Bank
228 Front St.
Plano, TX 75082

MEMO _____   _____

1:041000689:1   6066066 8' 304

Unit 9

> ## ► Do it yourself!
>
> **1.** Point. Talk about the people.
> *He likes the red tie.*
>
> **2.** Point. Ask your partner about the future.
> *Is she going to buy the suit?*
>
> **3.** Create conversations for the people.
> *A: Excuse me. How much is this tie?*
> *B: $7.99.*
>
> **4.** Say more about the picture. Use your <u>own</u> words. Say as much as you can.

Monday
6
NOVEMBER

Now I can
☐ talk about money.
☐ talk about the future.
☐ pay bills.
☐ write checks.
☐ use credit cards.
☐ _____.

Your career

➤ Vocabulary

Picture dictionary

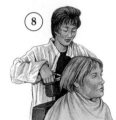

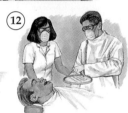

🎧 **A. Listen.**

Occupations and skills

1. a truck driver — drives a truck
2. a nurse's aide — helps nurses
3. a plumber — fixes toilets and sinks
4. a painter — paints houses
5. a telephone technician — installs telephones
6. a dishwasher — washes dishes

Occupations and skills

7. a cashier — uses a cash register
8. a hairdresser — cuts hair
9. a receptionist — greets visitors
10. a salesperson — sells
11. a child care worker — takes care of children
12. a dental assistant — helps dentists

Getting a job

13. a job application   14. an interview

🎧 **B. Listen again and repeat.**

🎧 **How to say it**

a child   children

C. Listen to the speakers. Circle the letter of the occupations.

1. **a.** a receptionist   **b.** a telephone technician
2. **a.** a plumber   **b.** a child care worker
3. **a.** a nurse's aide   **b.** a dishwasher
4. **a.** a painter   **b.** a hairdresser

D. Choose words. Write the words on the line.

1. Your _____ with Mr. Smith is at 11:00. Please be on time.

   interview / application

2. In order to apply for a job here, you need to fill out this job _____.

   application / interview

➤ Do it yourself!

A. Complete the chart. Then add your <u>own</u> skill and occupation. Or use the pictures.

Skills	Occupations
drive	*a truck driver, a bus driver*
wash dishes	
use a cash register	

a student, a teacher

a doctor, a nurse

a writer

a letter carrier

a sanitation worker

a paramedic

a firefighter

B. Pair work. What skill and occupation did <u>you</u> add? Tell your partner.

Practical conversations

Model 1 Talk about skills and experience.

A. Listen and read.

A: I'm looking for a job.
B: Good. What skills do you have?
A: Well, I can fix buses and trucks.
B: What was your last job?
A: I was a mechanic.
B: Do you want to fill out an application?
A: Yes, thanks.

B. Listen again and repeat.

C. Pair work. Use the information in the box. Then talk about your skills.

A: I'm looking for a job.
B: _____. What skills do you have?
A: Well, I can _____.
B: What was your last job?
A: I was _____.
B: Do you want to fill out an application?
A: _____.

Skills	Jobs
drive a bus	a bus driver
fix sinks	a plumber
wash dishes	a dishwasher
install telephones	a telephone technician

Model 2 Describe your personal qualities.

A. Listen and read.

A: Do you have any experience?
B: Well, not really. But I'm a good worker, and I learn fast.
A: That's great. Can you come for an interview tomorrow?
B: Sure.

B. Listen again and repeat.

C. Pair work. **Now use your <u>own</u> words.**

A: Do you have any experience?

B: Well, not really. But I'm a good worker, and I learn fast.

A: _____. Can you come for an interview _____?

B: _____.

Model 3   Ask about the past.

🎧 **A. Listen and read.**

A: So, Claudia, what did you do in Mexico?

B: Oh, me? I was a nurse.

A: A nurse! That's interesting! How long did you do that?

B: For four years. What about you? What did you do?

A: In China I was a homemaker.

🎧 **B. Listen again and repeat.**

C. Pair work. **Now talk about your <u>own</u> life.**

A: So, _____, what did you do in _____?

B: Oh, me? I was _____.

A: _____! That's interesting! How long did you do that?

B: _____. What about you? What did you do?

A: In _____ I was _____.

🎧 **Periods of time**

For four years.
From 1998 to 2001.

➤ **Do it yourself!**

A. Pair work. **Create a job interview from the picture. Talk about experience and skills. Use your <u>own</u> words.**

B. Personalization. **Work with a partner. Talk about your skills and experience. Ask and answer these questions.**

- What skills do you have?

- What did you do in your country?

- How long did you do that?

Do you have any experience?

Practical grammar

Talk about the past with <u>was</u>, <u>were</u>, <u>wasn't</u>, and <u>weren't</u>.

I
He   **was** a nurse for two years.
She

We
You   **were** nurses in China.
They

She **wasn't** at work on Monday. They **weren't** at school.

A. **Choose words. Write the words on the line.**

1. Francisco _____ a cook in his country. He was a restaurant manager.
   weren't / wasn't

2. Carol and Chen _____ receptionists from 1999 to 2000.
   was / were

3. Yong _____ a student in 1998. Now he's a child care worker.
   was / were

4. I _____ a dental assistant for seven years.
   was / were

5. We _____ dishwashers at Bill's Restaurant. We were cashiers.
   were / weren't

6. She _____ a technician. She was a nurse's aide.
   wasn't / weren't

Questions

Were you a cook in your country?	Yes, I **was**. / No, I **wasn't**.
How long **were** you a receptionist?	For three years.
Who **was** your manager?	Mr. Cortez.

B. **Choose words. Write the words on the line.**

1. Where _____ in 1998?
   they were / were they

2. When _____ a plumber?
   he was / was he

3. Who _____ at the supermarket?
   were / was

4. Why _____ in the hospital?
   you were / were you

5. _____ you at work yesterday?
   Were / Was

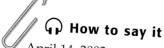

🎧 **How to say it**

April 14, 2002	=	today
April 13	=	yesterday
April 7–13	=	last week
March	=	last month
2001	=	last year

A: What **did** you **do** at your last job?
B: I **helped** customers.
A: **Did** you **use** a cash register?
B: Yes, I **did**. But I **didn't use** a computer.

🎧 **Regular past forms**

help	**helped**
wash	**washed**
fix	**fixed**
install	**installed**
use	**used**
paint	**painted**
greet	**greeted**

🎧 **Irregular past forms**

cut	**cut**
drive	**drove**
sell	**sold**
take	**took**

See page 140 for more irregular past forms.

C. **Write the simple past tense on the line.**

1. Last year we _____ the kitchen green.
   _{paint}

2. From 1997 to 1998, Carl _____ plumbing supplies, but now he's a plumber.
   _{sell}

3. I _____ at Broadway Hair Design for six months. First I was the
   _{work}
   receptionist, and then I _____ hair.
   _{cut}

4. Who _____ this microwave oven? Joe? He didn't clean the door!
   _{use}

5. Elena _____ the dishes in the kitchen. The sink was out of order.
   _{not wash}

➤ **Do it yourself!**

A. **Pair work. Ask and answer questions about the picture.**

A: *What was his last job?*
B: *He was a cashier.*

B. **Personalization. Ask your partner about himself or herself.**

A: *What did you do at your last job?*
B: *I painted houses.*

With words you know, YOU can talk to this dentist.

🎧 **A.** Listen and read.

Dentist: So, you're interested in the dental assistant opening at Family Dental Care.

YOU *Yes, I am.*

Dentist: That's great. We need several dental assistants right now. What kind of experience do you have?

YOU *Well, in Korea I was a dental assistant in a small dental office. Two dentists worked there.*

Dentist: Do you have experience as a dental assistant in this country?

YOU *Well, not really. But I'm a good worker, Dr. Martins.*

Dentist: Excellent. When would you be available to start work here at Family Dental Care?

YOU *In two weeks.*

🎧 **B.** Listen to the dentist. Read <u>your</u> part.

🎧 **C.** Listen and read. Choose <u>your</u> response. Circle the letter.

1. "I understand that you're interested in a job at Happy Holiday Hotels."

   a. Yes. I want to be an assistant manager.   **b.** That's interesting.

2. "What kind of experience do you have working in hotels?"

   a. I was a manager of a small hotel for three years.   **b.** I'm a good worker.

3. "When can you start work here?"

   a. From Monday to Friday.   **b.** In a week.

🎧 **D. Listen. Choose your response. Circle the letter.**

1. **a.** Is next Monday OK?　　**b.** From 1997 to 1999.

2. **a.** Not yet.　　**b.** In 1999.

3. **a.** Yes, I am.　　**b.** Let me check.

Listening comprehension

🎧 **A. Listen to the conversation. Then complete the sentences. Circle the letter.**

1. Ms. Miglin wants _____.　　**a.** a job　　**b.** some office supplies

2. Mr. Downs is a _____.　　**a.** store manager　　**b.** cashier

🎧 **B. Read the sentences. Then listen again. Write yes or no.**

1. Ms. Miglin wants a job as a cashier. _____

2. Ms. Miglin worked at Golden Office Supplies for six years. _____

3. Ms. Miglin has experience as a salesperson. _____

4. Ms. Miglin worked in the computer sales department. _____

5. Ms. Miglin can start work tomorrow. _____

➤ Do it yourself!

A. Write your own response. Then read your conversation out loud with a partner.

So, you're interested in working at this company.

YOU _____

What kind of experience do you have?

YOU _____

When can you start working here?

YOU _____

B. Discussion. Talk about an interview or about your last job.

Authentic practice 2

Reading

A. Read the ads. Answer the questions.

a

Company: Brown Construction Company
Position: Electrician's assistant
Experience required.
☑ Part-time   ☐ Full-time
Hours: 9:00 to 1:00

For an interview call 555-1000.

b Good Neighbor Direct • 4338 DiPaolo Center, Glenview IL 60025 • (800) 772-2229

FREE AD

Position: Housekeeper — Phone
Part-time
Hours: 7:00 to 12:00 — Phone
No experience required.
Apply at the 100 Garden — Phone
Street entrance.

Name Northview Hotel Date — Phone

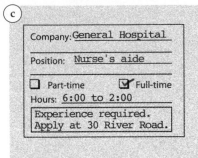

c

Company: General Hospital
Position: Nurse's aide
☐ Part-time   ☑ Full-time
Hours: 6:00 to 2:00
Experience required.
Apply at 30 River Road.

d Good Neighbor Direct • 4338 DiPaolo Center, Glenview IL 60025 • (800) 772-2229

FREE AD

Position: Plumber's helper — Phone
No experience required.
Driver's license required. — Phone
Full-time
Hours: 7:00 to 3:30 — Phone
Call 555-1234 for an
interview.
Name Express Date — Phone
    Plumbing

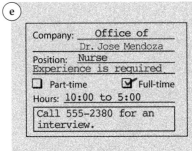

e

Company: Office of Dr. Jose Mendoza
Position: Nurse
Experience is required
☐ Part-time   ☑ Full-time
Hours: 10:00 to 5:00

Call 555-2380 for an interview.

f Good Neighbor Direct • 4338 DiPaolo Center, Glenview IL 60025 • (800) 772-2229

FREE AD

Position: Child care worker — Phone
No experience required.
Part-time — Phone
Hours: 3:30 to 6:00
Apply at 215 Bridge Street — Phone
after 2:30.

Name Child Care Center Date — Phone

1. How many jobs are full-time? _____

2. How many jobs require experience? _____

🎧 **Full-time and part-time**
full-time = 40 hours per week
part-time = under 40 hours,
    for example, 20 hours per week

B. Critical thinking. These people want jobs. Where can they apply? Write the letter of the ad.

Espinoza

1. Right now Rosa Espinoza is a homemaker. She has no job experience, but she can fix microwaves, lights, sinks, and toilets. She can fix cars and trucks, too. She has a driver's license. She needs a full-time job.

_____

Romano

2. Lisa Romano works at Best Supermarket every day from 8:00 to 2:00. She wants a part-time job. She likes to take care of children. She likes to cook and clean, too. _____

3. Jamal Salem was a nurse in his country. He can take a full-time or a part-time job. He has three small children. His wife's job starts at 4:00. Jamal needs to be home at 3:00 to take care of his children. _____

Salem

A. Ana Menendez filled out this job application for a job at the Northview Hotel. Read the application. Answer the questions.

Applicant: __Ana Menendez__   Position: __part-time housekeeper__

Employer or place	Job	Experience or skills	Dates
Mrs. Joan Crane 12 Ocean Drive Malibu, California	part-time housekeeper	I clean Mrs. Crane's house.	1/99 to now
In Peru I was a homemaker for 19 years.	full-time homemaker	I cooked, cleaned, and took care of my children.	1980 to 1999

1. What does Ms. Menendez do at her job? _____

2. What did she do from 1980 to 1999? What skills did she use? _____

_____

_____

B. Complete the application. Write about yourself.

Applicant: _____   Position: _____

Employer or place	Job	Experience or skills	Dates

> ➤ Do it yourself!   A plan-ahead project

Pair work. Bring in help-wanted ads from a newspaper. Choose a job. Practice your interview.

- Partner A is an interviewer.
- Partner B is a job applicant.

A. **Vocabulary. Complete the chart. Write a skill for each occupation.**

Occupation	Skill
1. hairdresser	
2. child care worker	
3. Your occupation:	

B. **Conversation. Choose your response. Circle the letter.**

1. "Do you have any experience?"

   a. Yes. I was a cashier in a clothes store. **b.** I'm looking for a job.

2. "That's great! How long did you do that?"

   a. In my country. **b.** For three years.

3. "Do you want to fill out an application?"

   a. I can learn fast. **b.** Yes, please.

C. **Grammar. Write the past tense form of the verb.**

1. Carlos ____*opened*____ the store at 9:00 this morning.
      open

2. At my old job, I _____ customers.
      greet

3. Who _____ your hair? It looks great!
      cut

4. How long _____ you a nurse's aide?
      be

5. I _____ that truck. Robert fixed it.
   not fix

D. **Reading. Read the ad. Then read about Alicia Fernandez. Can Ms. Fernandez apply for the job? Write yes or no.**

   Alicia Fernandez was a part-time truck driver in Mexico. She worked from 1998 to 1999. Now she's looking for a full-time job. _____

Company: Daily Bread Company

Position: Truck driver
5 years' experience
required.

☐ Part-time   ☑ Full-time

Hours: 7:00 to 3:00

Call 555-6300 for an
interview.

➤ Do it yourself!

1. Point. Talk about occupations and skills.
   He's a bus driver. He can drive a bus.

2. Point. Talk about the people.
   She filled out a job application.

3. Create conversations for the people.
   A: In Mexico I installed telephones.
   B: Do you have any experience here?

4. Say more about the picture. Use your <u>own</u> words. Say as much as you can.

Now I can
❑ talk about my skills and experience.
❑ talk about the past.
❑ interview for a job.
❑ fill out an application.
❑ _____.

Vocabulary reference lists

This is an alphabetical list of all active vocabulary in *Ready to Go 1*. The numbers refer to the page on which the word first appears. When a word has two meanings (a <u>can</u> of soup OR I <u>can</u> read), both are in the list.

paramedic   96
parking lot   24
partner   4
pay   108
pay by mail   108
paycheck   108
penny   109
people   24
person   24
personal day   90
phone number   5
picture   4
please   7
plumber   12
p.m.   62
point   1
post office   24
press   36

Q

quarter   109

R

read   1
ready   86
really   75
receipt   48
receptionist   120
recipe   81
red   48
refrigerator   74
refund   56
repeat   1
restaurant   24
restroom   24
return   54
rice   72
right   26
right now   15

S

salesperson   48
sanitation worker   121
schedule   68
school   24
sell   120
sentence   4
she   16
shelf   75
shirt   48
shoes   48

shopping   108
sink   120
sister   84
size   50
skill   120
skirt   48
small   50
sometimes   100
son   84
start   39
stay home   84
store   48
student   12
study   84
sugar   72
suit   48
supermarket   24
supply room   24

T

take (medicine)   97
take care of   120
talk   1
tea   72
teacher   4
telephone   36
telephone number   45
telephone technician   120
that   53
the   26
their   100
there is   77
there are   77
these   53
they   28
think   51
this   53
those   53
tie   48
time   60
time card   61
to   *prep.*   2
to (until)   123
today   60
toilet   120
tomato   72
tomorrow   60
too   51
truck   120
truck driver   120
turn   36

U

unemployed   15
uniform   48
unplug   36
use   120

V

visitor   120

W

want   52
was   124
wash   120
water   72
we   28
week   60
well   15
were   124
what   28
what color   50
what size   50
what time   62
when   62
where   26
white   48
who   28
whose   112
why   87
why not   86
wife   84
word   4
work *n.*   29
work *v.*   84
worker   122
wrist   96
write   1
writer   121
wrong   51

Y

year   60
yellow   48
yes   6
yesterday   124
yet   87
you *sing.*   16
you *pl.*   28
your   100

Z

zip code   5

This is a unit-by-unit list of all the social language from the practical conversations in *Ready to Go 1*.

Welcome to *Ready to Go*

Hello.
I'm Carmen.
Hi.
Nice to meet you.
Nice to meet you too.
Mary, this is John. John, this is Mary.
Is that M-A-R-Y? (for clarification)
What's your name, please?
Is that your first name?
And what's your last name?
Thank you.
What's your address?
Is that 30 or 13? (for clarification)
Thanks.
You're welcome.
What's your phone number?
And your area code?

Unit 1

Are you Ken Wang?
Yes, I am./No, I'm not.
Oh, hi.
Good to meet you.
Where are you from?
What about you?
What do you do?
And you?
Oh, I'm sorry. (to express sympathy)
Well, good luck!

Unit 2

Excuse me? (to ask for repetition)
Excuse me. (to initiate a conversation)
I'm looking for the _____.
The _____? (to ask for clarification)

Unit 3

Oh, no! (to express dismay)
What's wrong?
Let's _____ (as in How do I _____?) (for suggestions)
Good idea.
OK. No problem. (to agree to a command)
How do I _____? (to ask for directions)
OK. (to express comprehension)
I don't know.

Unit 4

Sure. (to express willingness)
OK. (to express willingness)
This way, please.
I'm sorry. (to apologize)
May I help you?
Yes, please.
Yes, I think so.

Unit 5

What time is it?
Uh-oh. (to express dismay)
Bye.
See you later.
I'm not sure.
_____, I think. (to express an opinion)
That's great! (to express enthusiasm)

Unit 6

What's up?
Not much.
Anything else?
No, that's all.
Not me.
What about milk?
Me too!
We're out of _____.

Unit 7

Not yet.
OK. (to express permission)
Well, _____. (to introduce a thought)

Unit 8

Hello? (to answer the telephone)
This is Bill. (telephone identification)
Can you talk?
Can I call you back?
Sure. No problem. (to agree to a request)
Talk to you later.
How can I help you? (formal telephone answering)
How about 10:30? (to agree to a time)
That's fine. (to agree to a date)
See you then.
Feel better!
Thanks a lot.
It's on its way.

Unit 9

Do you have change for twenty dollars?
Let me check.
Here you go.
How much is this _____? (to ask for a price)
That's a lot. (to respond to a price)
I'll have to think about it.
Only $85. (to suggest that a price is low)
It's on sale.
I'll take it. (to agree to buy)
Will that be cash or charge?

Unit 10

I'm looking for a job.
What was your last job?
Do you want to fill out an application?
Do you have any experience?
Well, not really.
So, _____? (to introduce a question)
Oh, me?
That's interesting!

Irregular verbs

The following verbs from *Ready to Go 1* have irregular past-tense forms.

Verb	Past-tense form
be	was / were
buy	bought
can	could
come	came
cut	cut
do	did
drink	drank
drive	drove
eat	ate
go	went
have	had
hurt	hurt
know	knew
make	made
meet	met
pay	paid
read	read
sell	sold
take	took
think	thought
write	wrote

Days

Monday	Friday
Tuesday	Saturday
Wednesday	Sunday
Thursday	

Months

January	July
February	August
March	September
April	October
May	November
June	December

Numbers

Cardinal numbers

1	one	16	sixteen
2	two	17	seventeen
3	three	18	eighteen
4	four	19	nineteen
5	five	20	twenty
6	six	21	twenty-one
7	seven	30	thirty
8	eight	40	forty
9	nine	50	fifty
10	ten	60	sixty
11	eleven	70	seventy
12	twelve	80	eighty
13	thirteen	90	ninety
14	fourteen	100	one hundred
15	fifteen	200	two hundred

1,000	one thousand
1,000,000	one million
1,000,000,000	one billion

Ordinal numbers

first	seventeenth
second	eighteenth
third	nineteenth
fourth	twentieth
fifth	twenty-first
sixth	twenty-second
seventh	thirtieth
eighth	thirty-first
ninth	fortieth
tenth	fiftieth
eleventh	sixtieth
twelfth	seventieth
thirteenth	eightieth
fourteenth	ninetieth
fifteenth	hundredth
sixteenth	thousandth

Following are lists of additional words to expand the vocabulary of each unit. These optional word lists contain a maximum of 20 words.

Unit 1

More countries and nationalities

These are the 20 largest recent immigrant groups.

If your country or nationality isn't here, write it on the lines at the bottom of the list.

China	Chinese
Colombia	Colombian
Cuba	Cuban
Dominican Republic	Dominican
El Salvador	Salvadoran
Greece	Greek
Guatemala	Guatemalan
Haiti	Haitian
India	Indian
Iran	Iranian
Jamaica	Jamaican
Korea	Korean
Mexico	Mexican
Philippines	Filipino
Poland	Polish
Portugal	Portuguese
Russia	Russian
Taiwan	Taiwanese
Ukraine	Ukrainian
Vietnam	Vietnamese

_____   _____
<u>My</u> country   <u>My</u> nationality

Where do your classmates come from? List any other countries and nationalities.

_____   _____

_____   _____

_____   _____

Unit 2

More places

an adult school
a college
a daycare center
a high school

a barber shop
a beauty shop

a movie theater
a shopping mall

a church
a mosque
a synagogue
a temple

an auto repair shop
a bus station
a factory
a garage
a laundromat
a library
a train station
a warehouse

Unit 3

More equipment and machines

a cassette player
a CD player
a conveyor
a drill
a dryer
a forklift
a hammer
an iron
a jackhammer
a lathe
a power saw
a radio
a saw
a screwdriver

a sewing machine
a shovel
a stove
a TV
a washing machine

Unit 4

More stores

an auto parts store
a bookstore
a bakery
a candy store
a car dealership
a computer store
a convenience store
a department store
a discount store
a drugstore
an electronics store
a florist
a grocery store
a hardware store
an office supply store
a paint store
a plumbing supply store
a secondhand store
a shoe store
a video store

Unit 5

More time telling

three ten
ten after three
ten after
ten past three
ten past

three fifteen
a quarter after three
a quarter after
a quarter past three
a quarter past

three thirty
half past three
half past

three forty-five
a quarter to four
a quarter to
a quarter of four
a quarter of

Unit 6

More foods

butter
yogurt

a banana
an orange
a peach
a pear

broccoli
a pea
a potato

a pita
a tortilla

a cake
a cookie
a pie

ketchup
mustard
oil
pepper
salt
vinegar

Unit 7

More family members

a baby
an uncle
an aunt
a nephew
a niece
a cousin

a grandfather
a grandmother
a grandson
a granddaughter

a father-in-law
a mother-in-law
a son-in-law
a daughter-in-law
a brother-in-law
a sister-in-law

a stepfather
a stepmother
a stepson
a stepdaughter
a stepbrother
a stepsister

Unit 8

More body parts

a chest
an elbow
a finger
a fingernail
hair
a knee
a shoulder
a toe
a waist

a cheek
an ear
an eye
a face
a mouth
a nose
a tongue
a tooth

Unit 9

More documents

a birth certificate
a business card
a debit card
a fare card
a green card
an insurance card
a library card
a passport
a state I.D. card
a student I.D. card
a traveler's check
a visa
a work authorization permit

Unit 10

More occupations

a barber
a beautician
a busboy
a carpenter
a construction worker
a doorman
a file clerk
a florist
a gardener
a janitor
a locksmith
an optician
an orderly
a seamstress
a security guard
a stock clerk
a tailor
a teller
a travel agent
a waiter / waitress

My address book

Name _____   Telephone (_____)_____

Address _____

Name _____   Telephone (_____)_____

Address _____

Name _____   Telephone (_____)_____

Address _____

Name _____   Telephone (_____)_____

Address _____

Name _____   Telephone (_____)_____

Address _____

Name _____   Telephone (_____)_____

Address _____

My address book

Name _____   Telephone (_____)_____

Address _____

Name _____   Telephone (_____)_____

Address _____

Name _____   Telephone (_____)_____

Address _____

Name _____   Telephone (_____)_____

Address _____

Name _____   Telephone (_____)_____

Address _____

Name _____   Telephone (_____)_____

Address _____

My address book

Name _____   Telephone (_____)_____

Address _____

Name _____   Telephone (_____)_____

Address _____

Name _____   Telephone (_____)_____

Address _____

Name _____   Telephone (_____)_____

Address _____

Name _____   Telephone (_____)_____

Address _____

Name _____   Telephone (_____)_____

Address _____